To:
Holley
Thank
for
your
Support

IT'S OKAY
TO CRY

When the Odds are Against You

Lynne L Jasames MBA

Printed in the United States
Editor: Linda Hall

Forward Edit: Sumaya Brown
Art Design: Ricky Scott Holmes

Book Cover Design: Creating Genius
ISBN: 0989744906
ISNB 13: 9780989744904

DEDICATION

I dedicate this book to all those who are trying to find peace, purpose and understanding when traumatic, devastating and hurtful things happen in life. It's how you respond to those things, how you live through those things, and what you learn from those things, that makes life worth embracing.

EXPRESSION

This book was not written to offend, hurt, or ruin anyone's character. These are my experiences in my relationships with people in my life. This is my interpretation of how each situation and/or circumstance contributed to the woman I am today.

ACKNOWLEDGEMENTS

I would like to thank God for Peace. It is while seeking peace that pain, shame, guilt, anger, and frustration could be released and growth, love, happiness, compassion, and forgiveness could enter my heart.

I would like to thank my children for their love. Love removed fear and gave me strength, motivation and determination to get back up whenever I felt like I couldn't keep going.

I want to thank my team. There are those that provided insight, motivated me, made edits, critiqued, never gave up on me during the journey and smiled during the changing due dates. Patrick Clark II, Michael Durant, Makeva Walker, Les Brown, Sumaya Brown, Linda Hall, Wanda Clark, Mark Fierro, and Dustin Gold. I could not do this by myself.

"I'm a success today because I had a friend who believed in me and I didn't have the heart to let him down."

~Abraham Lincoln

FOREWORD BY LES BROWN

Did you know that you are far more capable of overcoming challenges than you realize? You are designed to be resilient! Regardless of what it looks like, you will do more than survive. You will conquer! I have a saying that "When life knocks you down, try and land on your back because if you can look up; you can get up!" No one on this earth can control "the hand that they are dealt" in life. Lynne Jasames certainly didn't have a choice. As a teenage mother, Lynne endured many challenges that left her broken and longing for brighter days. Through perseverance and determination, Lynne resolved within herself that she would not be a victim or a statistic. Lynne is a triumphant survivor. She stands strong, using her story as a beacon of hope and empowerment. As an author, motivational speaker and mentor, Lynne shares her message of strength to audiences nationwide. Lynne is a firm believer that anyone can beat the odds. In "When the Odds are Against You", Lynne provides experiential wisdom and insights that will compel you to push beyond the tears and trying circumstances. Are you going through hardships? Have you fallen on difficult times? Are you in the midst of a turbulent storm? Each chapter leads us down a path of how to turn tears into determination, courage, and becoming unstoppable. Lynne is a dedicated mother of five children, who chooses to live an exceptional life and initiate a work that will inspire people to live their dreams. Lynne is a shining example that what happens to you does not matter as much as what happens in you. She's proven time and time again that when life drops you to your knees, pray as if everything depends upon God, but work as if everything depends upon you. Lynne believes that all of us should adopt the mindset that giving up is not an option and that we have to affirm within ourselves that "it's not over until I win!"

Teen Pregnancy

Parenthood is the leading reason that teen girls drop out of school. More than 50% of teen mothers never graduate from high school. Less than 2% of teen moms earn a college degree by age 30.

Only one-third of teenage mothers completes high school and receives their diplomas. By age 30, only 1.5 percent of women who had pregnancies as a teenager have a college degree. 80 percent of unmarried teen mothers end up on welfare. Sons of teenaged mothers have a 13 percent greater chance of ending up in prison as compared to their peers.

There were the facts, the rumors and the people that know it all that said because I was a teen mother I would drop out of high school. There is no way I would obtain a college degree. I would raise my children on welfare and because I was a teen mother my children and I would be socially disadvantaged. My children would do poorly in school, and my children have a greater chance of being abused and/or neglected. Unfortunately, male children born to teen mothers are more likely to serve time in prison, compared to their peers. I have heard that children who are raised in a family of addicts are more likely to become addicts as well. I was called nasty, the whore, the girl that did it all the time. I was fass' and wouldn't grow up to be anything. I was no longer an innocent little girl.

Teen Mothers

As a teen parent be prepared to give up hanging out with your friends and doing what teens without children can do socially. You must take total responsibility for YOUR child. You should not expect any relative or friend to help you unless it is absolutely necessary. Yes, you will need help, however you should not ask for help when you want to party, hang out with your friends, or go to sleep because you are too tired from activities that will not improve you or your child's lives. You decided to have a baby, not your family or friends. The idea of the situation being fun and easy becomes a harsh reality. The baby shower was nice and the gifts were fabulous. Your friends even promised to help you. You probably thought you would be with the father forever. The reality is you are bringing another person into this world and you are not even old enough or prepared to take care of yourself. Most teens do not consider all the responsibilities that will rest on their shoulders. The decision gets real when you think long term about the future for you and your child. Everyone who is laughing with you and encouraging you will not be there in the long run. Trust me I know, because I did not think about these things when I became pregnant with my children.

When I saw the statistics I just cried about the future of my children and me. I told myself I would do everything to prove these statistics wrong. I made up my mind that I would be better than every negative thing a person or statistic said about me. I knew I was better than that. I looked into my children's eyes and got stronger. I was determined to give them a better life. My journey was hard. Any teenager with no children has a better chance at success, but it does not mean that a teen parent cannot be successful. I made the same mistake more than once. The truth is, I was immature, irresponsible, did not live in reality and listened to other immature people. Being a teen parent does not define you or your future. It's an opportunity to prove to those that do not see your greatness just how great you are.

Foster Children

Less than 3% go to college. 51% are unemployed. Emancipated females are 4 times more likely to receive public assistance than the general population. In any given year, foster children compromise less than 0.3% of the state's population, and yet 40% of persons living in homeless shelters are former foster children. A similarly disproportionate percentage of the nation's prison population is comprised of former foster youth.

Being a foster child and knowing that each month more than 2,000 young people age out of foster care without having a permanent family or home was discouraging. Within two years of leaving foster care many of these children will be homeless, incarcerated, or unemployed. Foster children are more than likely to do poorly in school, abuse or neglect their children, and be socially disadvantaged. It was heart breaking to hear what people thought they knew about foster children. It was devastating at times to hear what the mean people had to say about foster children. To have such labels like; bad, dumb, unwanted, won't grow up to be anybody, ugly, dirty, stupid, can't read or write, throw away and so much more can either make you stronger or break up down.

Foster Sisters and Brothers

We all entered the foster care system for different reasons. We were removed from our parents or caregiver. In that moment for me, my ability to trust shifted. My world came clashing down and I could not control what was happening. I shared these feelings with many foster children during my journey. We have a connection that changed our lives from the day we were removed and entered foster care. We learned to take responsibility for our siblings and ourselves. We had to become the parent to our parents and siblings in some cases. We lost our ability to trust openly and had to learn to survive faster than our peers. We know we have to keep looking forward and not look back. We have to develop an attitude about who we were, who we wanted to become, and decided that nothing would stop us from overcoming the stereotypes, the hearsay, the myths, or the statistics. We have to constantly prove that we could be somebody. We faced challenges that our peers would not understand unless they have been through the same process.

While in foster care, I told myself daily that my circumstances would not always be this way because eventually I would turn eighteen years old. I told myself daily that I could be somebody and not become a statistic. I refused to turn to drugs, alcohol, anger, or the streets for comfort. I refused to do what was the expected norm for a foster child. I was determined to prove statistics, the gossipers, those who did not understand, and those who doubted me wrong. I also wanted to make proud all those who believed in me, who hung in there with me and gave me a chance. Be a foster child to the world but a miracle child in your own heart. Face the challenges that come your way with your head up and believe that this time in your life is a time to get stronger and know there's a purpose along your journey.

INTRODUCTION

"The struggle of my life created empathy- I could relate to pain, being abandoned, having people not love me."

~Oprah Winfrey

I lived a life of uncertainty and doubt for as long as I can remember. As a child I did not understand my life. I gave myself excuses, reasons and explanations when bad things happened to me. I questioned my life and asked God why I had to have a drug addicted mother and grow up without my father. I needed to know why I ended up in foster care. Why I struggled in relationships. Why was I molested? I never really understood why I had to be a teen mother. I needed to know why and continue to ask God a million questions. I often cried, asked, and begged God for answers. I even had the nerve to demand that He be clear with His response.

I did not know if I was dreaming, thinking too hard, or what. One day, I heard God telling an angel that he had to create a girl that could handle every adversity he placed before her. He insisted that she would be born into a family of addicts that included her mother. He told the angel "she would be a teen mother, would give birth to five sons and that she would have her first child at the tender age of fourteen. Three of her sons would be born before she turned eighteen. She would endure physical, mental and sexual abuse and would age out of the foster care system. At the age of twelve, a man in his twenties would have sex with her. Her father would die before she turned one year old. This girl would be strong despite all obstacles."

"Although she would be born into a family of addicts, she would not become one. She would go through several relationships that would give her the strength and emotions to fulfill her destiny in adulthood. These emotions and trials would make her stronger even though she would not understand the path chosen for her. She would struggle, be disappointed a lot, and have hard times. In spite of all that, she would live a blessed life. She would give her heart away over and over until the right man was placed in her life. She would help people just because her heart told her to, and not expect anything in return. She would raise her sons in a society that predicted she could not raise her sons as a single mother. Her tears would be her way of releasing her pain and take the place of drugs and alcohol. These tears would give her strength. She would defy all statistics and succeed without making excuses for failure." I heard the angel ask, "Why would so many odds be against her?" God answered and said, "I know she will be able to handle it." I started crying and continued to ask God, "Why me?"

I struggled with trying to understand what God thought he could do with me. I wondered what was so special about me. I gave birth to my first child while I was still a child myself. I was a child that nobody could imagine would get an education and become successful. Society would predict that I would have a bunch of babies, raise my children on government assistance, live in the projects, and raise a bunch of gang banging sons, who would spend their time in the juvenile justice system or in prison. I grew up struggling with trying to understand who I was. I wondered why I was here and why I had to go through all my struggles. I desperately needed to know why these things happened to the skinny black girl that grew up thinking she had a fair complexion.

I often searched for something that would add meaning to my tears. I tried to understand why I cried so much. I became tired of the tears and no longer wanted to feel weak as a result of crying. I needed something to relate to. I received the same story in e-mail over and over again. Eventually, I paid close attention and took my time while reading it several times. The story became personal to me. In some way, I felt stronger and encouraged. The title was "Why Women Cry."

Why Women Cry

One day a little boy asked his mother, "Why are you crying?" "Because I'm a woman," she told him. "I don't understand," said the little boy. His Mother just hugged him and said, "And you never will." Later the little boy asked his father, "Why does mother seem to cry all the time for no reason?" His father's reply was "All women cry, all the time, for no reason." That was all his dad could say to the little boy. The little boy grew up and became a man. As he aged he wondered why women cry. Finally he got on his knees and prayed to God. When he felt a connection with God, he asked, "God, why do women cry so easily?" God said, "When I made the woman she had to be Special. I made her shoulders strong enough to carry the weight of the world, yet gentle enough to give comfort. I gave her an inner strength to endure childbirth and the rejection that many times will come from her children. I gave her a hardness that allows her to keep going when everyone else gives up on her. She will take care of her family through sickness and fatigue without complaining. I gave her the sensitivity to love her children under any and all circumstances, even when her child has hurt her very badly. I gave her strength to carry her husband through his faults and fashioned her from his rib to protect his heart. I gave her wisdom to know that a good husband never hurts his wife, but sometimes tests her strengths and her resolve to stand beside him unfalteringly.

And finally, I gave her a tear to shed. This is hers exclusively to use whenever it is needed." "You see my son," said God, "the beauty of a woman is not in the clothes she wears, the figure that she carries, or the way she combs her hair. The beauty of a woman must be seen in her eyes, because that is the doorway to her heart - a place where her love resides."

Of course I was crying by the time I got to the end. I know Maya Angelo had some part of this message.

I did not know what I would be when I grew up or how my life would turn out. As a child, I did not think that I would have a college degree. I did not think I would have five children or that three of them would be born before I left high school. In spite of everything, we turned out better than statistics said we would. I have not married yet but I have some very good men in my life, genuinely good male friends, and five handsome sons. I ended up in foster care, but made it through that part of my life without giving up. My mother is on drugs, but I love her and will always be here for her. One of my sisters and I do not have a solid relationship, but I carry her in my heart and love her very much. One of my aunts was shot and killed while my mother and sisters and I were in the house. I survived that shooting and the shooting of my younger sister. I purchased my first home on my own and my sons have made me a proud mother, over and over again.

As a child I learned about God from people who shared their perspectives with me about the bible and how to live a religious life. Unfortunately, I was not taught about having inner peace. I struggled with right and wrong. As I got older I realized "Church" people are often the most judgmental. I grew up believing that if I followed a straight and narrow path, did things a certain way, my life would turn out so much better. All I had to do was follow the rules society said I should follow, how the church said I should act or how I should be, or what was set forth in the bible (from somebody else's perspective), and just pray to God and ask for forgiveness. I had to be an honest and trust worthy person with lots of integrity. I could not lie or steal and never do anything I would not want done to me. I had to help people and be a loving and kind person at all times. I have those attributes and I embrace them. I believed that if I were a good person it would all come back to me. Those beliefs were far from the truth. I realized I have a lot of good qualities without attending church or having someone tell me how to live my life. I have peace.

While working on this book on July 10, 2012, I read a post by Tyler Perry on Face Book. He wrote about the times he had questions for God. I realized other people question God and its okay.

> *"It doesn't matter if a million people tell you what you can't do, or if ten million tell you no. If you get one yes from God, that's all you need. "*

> **~ Tyler Perry**

Something to Think About

I saw someone I remembered from high school. We had an interesting conversation that brought up old feelings and emotions. I could not remember her name until she started talking. She gave me a big hug that felt genuine. She had heard a lot about my life and me since our high school days. She knew I worked full time for the County and that I had bought a big four-bedroom house with a pool all by myself. She described my fancy car with nice rims. She knew my sons wore name brand clothing and shoes all the time. I wondered where she got that information and why I was important enough to be talked about. She filled me in on other friends that were not doing well in their careers, or with their families. She spoke about whose children had become juvenile delinquents or were in same sex relationships. I was surprised when she told me she would love to be in my shoes. I said to her, "What if I cried myself to sleep last night?" She was puzzled by the question. I told her what goes on behind closed doors is not evident to the public. I cry more than people can imagine. I smile and put on a happy face so no one can see the pain and suffering I have endured. I let her know that without prayer and faith I would not have succeeded. She said she heard I had a very cute boyfriend who treated me with utmost respect. I said, "Really, is that what you heard?" She laughed a little and continued by saying everyone thought we made a very cute couple and that we would be getting married soon. I looked at her, smiled and said, "I am no longer with him." She was stunned. She continued by telling me that throughout the years people told her what they knew about my glamorous life. They all seemed to know about my children, my relationships and about me going to college. I felt ill while listening to her talking about my last relationship. She heard it was a very good one. What she did not know was how I had a hard time looking in the mirror that morning and I did not want to get out of bed because I was feeling very lonely. She complimented me on how good I looked considering I had four children. When I told her that I was sucking in my stomach and my bra made my breasts look very perky, all she could do was laugh with me. She had nothing else to say after that. I was glad our paths had crossed. We exchanged numbers and said our good byes.

She, along with several other former high school friends and people from the projects, usually said similar things about my family and me. They would say how good they thought my life was, and how they would love to be in my shoes. I heard about how I was doing this and doing that, my favorite is, "Girl, you still working two and three jobs?" I would just smile and say, "I do what I have to do." Their response was usually, "You are crazy and I do not see how you do it." I heard about how well behaved my handsome boys were, that they were good students and athletes, how they are close and that they stick together. They are glad to hear Patrick went away to college to play basketball. I just listen while trying not to cry, as I reflected on what they were saying and how good it all sound. I respond with much appreciation while listening to what was going on in their lives and I gave encouraging words as best I could. Sometimes I would give advice about family, relationships, and children. When I reflect on my own life I end up crying while thanking God that I remained strong, and never gave up. I begged for more strength to continue on the path I have started. People only know what they have heard, what they think they know about me and what they see on the outside.

I have learned that people have no idea what's behind a smiling face. A lot of people have unfortunate and heartbreaking stories about their lives. You can look into someone's face and believe they have the life you dreamed of having. You might be one of those people, just like I was. You can believe you would give up your life to have another person's life. People do not carry their life story on their face. You see the smile, the good job, the fancy car, the name brand clothes, the big house, beautiful children, and you see the happy "looking" couple. Have you ever wondered what was behind that smile or that smirk you saw today? Have you? Do they smile daily? Do they look happy all the time? What can make a person smile today, and cry tomorrow? Can it be because they thought about something that happened to them yesterday or even when they were younger? Did they really have a perfect life? Do they have the life that many people dream about? Do I have a life that people think they would trade for theirs? Maybe you thought you wanted that life until you learned things about that person you did not know or had not heard about before. People's lives are not always what they appear to be. I'm not sure I could handle things that have happened in somebody else's life. That's why we all have our own journey with obstacles that God knows we can handle.

When people look at me, they see a smile or a laugh. What they do not know is that more than likely I cried myself to sleep the night before or that my stomach hurts sometimes from fears of failing, stressing and worrying. Even though things appear very good on the surface, no one knows my entire story. People do not know the depth of my pain, the things I have experienced, witnessed or the obstacles I have overcome. I have faced many challenges and through it all, I was determined to stay strong. My face tells nothing about how I'm feeling or what's going on with me. I smile and laugh all the time. Those smiles are to brighten somebody else's day and help me push through mine. I am truly blessed, and the blessings are appreciated because of the hard times I struggled through. I have cried more than laughed and have had many hurtful life experiences. I have been what society said I should be. I gave when I did not have anything left to give and I sacrificed from my children and myself over and over again to help other people. I was loyal even in the face of adversity. I gave respect when it was not earned or deserved. I still believed when my faith was at its weakest. I let people know I appreciated them and went above and beyond to show it. My son wonders why I continue to do the "right thing", even though life appears to have not been fair to me.

With all my challenges, I have survived with God's grace, the love of my children, and determination that comes from the pit of my stomach. It is my hope that you are able to read what I am sharing with an open mind. I know many of us share these same feelings. I would like for you to learn from my story and use my examples when you need to get out of an unhealthy situation, press forward when you don't feel like it, and continue to desire better for yourself. If at all possible, do not let any obstacles keep you from attaining your dreams or goals. Keep in mind challenges usually make us stronger, they are learning experiences. It is important to be surrounded by positive and uplifting people and to follow their lead. I asked a lot of questions, paid close attention and gathered the information I needed to become the successful woman I am today. I still have a lot of work to do and much more to accomplish.

"Every great dream begins with a dreamer. Always remember, you have within you the

strength, the patience, and the passion to reach for the stars to change the world."

~Harriet Tubman

Most people have a story to share that could possibly help others become stronger. I want people to realize that they are not the only one who has been through heartache, pain, suffering, betrayal, and doubt. I have learned that there are others in situations that were a lot worse than my own. I tell my story hoping that the right woman or girl can read it and find herself in a better place. My high school friend only talked about what she heard. She had no idea what trials and tribulations I had gone through to get where I am today. One day I met a man in a training class who wore a nice suit and appeared to be calm and collected. His facial expression was inviting which made it seem okay to sit at the table with him without feeling I was invading his space. He told me that his son was in the hospital having surgery on his face because he tried to commit suicide by shooting himself under his chin. The bullet went through his face, never touching his brain. I was reminded that my "pity parties" were nothing compared to what I could be going through. His story changed my attitude about things that were happening in my life. How I viewed things in my life, and I realized that my troubles could only make me stronger. I had always endured my struggles and was determined to get pass them now. There are other woman and girls going through so much more than I have.

I have always been proud of the fact that I do not give up easily. There have been times when I thought I could not continue. Somehow, I managed to hold my head up high and faced all of the adversity that came my way. Once I turned thirty, fighting was not as easy as it had been. As my boys aged and needed me less, my motivation started decreasing. After going through so much, I felt like life was becoming too much to handle. The feeling of emptiness took a toll on me mentally. I suffered several inner breaking points. Friends made my life sound too good to be true. Growing up with so much negativity made me fail to see the good at times.

When I met Busta, I thought my good deeds of giving to others, being loyal and a good person had finally paid off in the area of relationships. I remember thinking that I had found my soul mate. Well my soul mate was not what I thought he was. My financial, emotional, physical, and spiritual support was not enough for him. He left me feeling lonely and confused. I gave him energy that he did not deserve. That emptiness without him was sickening and left me unable to function at my normal capacity. I felt like I did not want to live without him. It was ironic how I had always had the answer for someone else in an emotional relationship, but did not know how to help myself. Relationships are a choice. Busta was a choice. I have so much more to focus on and give good energy to than Busta. I learned that because I put so much of myself into him, I felt lost once he was gone. I know now that I can be with a man and stay true to myself at the same time. The fact that I was so focused on him, my goals and dreams were lost at the time. I have accomplished so much since I ended that relationship. My hope is that anyone in a toxic relationship can see themselves in my behavior, call me stupid because then they will see their stupidity and make changes in their relationship.

When it comes to life and relationships I agree Albert.

> *"You have to learn the rules of the game. And then you have to play better than anyone else."*

> ~ **Albert Einstein**

WHY

1

PAIN

I was born in Los Angeles, California and raised in Las Vegas, Nevada. I have two sisters, Desire' (Dimples) is oldest and Rise' (Precious) is the youngest, I am Lynne (Special) the middle child. My father reportedly died of an asthma attack in LA County jail before my first birthday. One of my first memories of my mother leaving us alone was the day she went to prison. After that, my sisters and I lived with my grandfather in Las Vegas. The rest of my family lived in California. I was confused and I do not remember how old I was. Life seemed so unfair to me and there was nothing I could do about it. Since granddaddy had to work, my sisters and I stayed with his friend. We really did not know granddaddy so we did whatever we were told and kept quiet. Our new baby sitter was very nice when granddaddy came around. We were treated very badly when he was not there. She yelled at us all the time for no reason. We could not express ourselves or talk without getting into trouble. I do not remember going to school. I am almost positive my granddaddy was paying her, but back in those days children definitely stayed out of grown folk's business. We were forced to eat beans almost at every single meal. Sometime we had hot dogs or cereal, but most of the time we ate little brown beans.

If granddaddy brought us something, the babysitter took it away and gave it to her children. The things she did not take, her children broke. I remember crying because nothing was done about it. When we told granddaddy, the babysitter would say we broke the toys or we lost them. We were yelled at since she was believed and we were not. He even threatened not buy us anything else. I remember the day we got a bouncy ball. We were so happy and loved that ball. Later that night, the sitter's daughter squeezed all the air out. I just stared at her and cried myself to sleep. The next day the lady told her friend how bad we were and how she did not like us for reasons we never understood. When my mother came home I vividly remember her saying she would never leave us again. I am not sure if my mother knew we were not living with granddaddy while she was away. We never moved back to California.

When momma returned from prison, life seemed fair again and I believed my life would be perfect from then on. Years later momma was injured in a car accident and started taking prescription medication. My family did not know it yet, but that was when life for us started going downhill. We eventually moved to the projects. Most people have their own perception of what living in the projects is like. There are myths and stereotypes. Project life was much different from living in a house because everyone knew our business and there was little or no privacy. We were often asked to lend or had to borrow items from toilet tissue, to sugar and even clothes. There were more people to talk about you and more people to please or become our enemy. Throughout those years, I watched my mother become more and more addicted to drugs. I watched my oldest sister fight other girls because of gossip and jealousy. I watched how friends played one against the other and boyfriends were shared behind each other's back. Because I was trusted, I knew a lot of people's business. I watched my so-called friends come and go. They would be angry with me one minute and be my best friend the next. The females in the projects became "Auntie So and So" my God Sisters, God Mothers or my cousins. Every Christmas and school year I watched my friends get everything they wanted and needed while at times we got nothing at all. I learned at an early age that I desired more for myself and wanted a much better life. One Christmas momma sat us down and explained why we would not get presents that year. I looked her in the face and said I understood and that it was okay. I went downstairs and cried myself to sleep that Christmas Eve and cried hard. It was sad that the tree had no presents under it. When I woke up the next morning I heard knocking on the door. I just lay there on the couch afraid to move, because I could hear my so-called friends talking about my sisters and me. I heard them going on and on about how we did not get anything for Christmas. It hurt me deep down in my soul to hear what they were saying. I was very angry and I made another vow to always do better for my children than my mother had done for us.

As years passed, times became much harder because momma became heavily addicted to drugs. My favorite auntie, who always helped us out, got murdered leaving us without the support we often depended on. She was the relative who had her head on straight and took care of us when momma messed up.

Eventually, I had to live with various friends and wore handed down clothes. I hated wearing the same pants and rotating different shoes and shirts weekly, hoping my friends would not notice. I remember a conversation between two friends about name brand clothing. One of them was saying she was getting another color of Levi jeans and the other one was commenting on making her Levi's into straight legs. I stood their wondering what Levi's were. I did not know and it drove me crazy. I knew it was something that I did not have. I remember all my friends wearing EBS shoes that I never got. That is when I had developed an understanding about name brand clothing that my sisters and I never had. We did not know what a shopping mall was and only shopped at Zodys and K-Mart. That lowered my self-esteem and I made another vow to do better in life for myself, and my children. I did not want to go to school since I did not have decent clothes to wear.

When I started taking interest in boys my self-esteem sank even lower. I thought all the boys liked my friend with the long hair and lighter skin. She got everything when it was time to shop for school, Christmas, her birthday, and sometimes just because. I told myself it was because my friend had her mother and her father in her life. As soon as a guy took interest in my body I thought I was liked. I began to do what I thought it took to make a guy like me. Sex became my way of feeling like somebody cared.

Our spiritual guidance started when Grandma Addie insisted on my sisters and me attending Vacation Bible School every summer. We hated going to Bible School, but we had no choice. The other children were so mean and talked about us loud enough for us to hear them. I thought maybe it was because we did not attend their church on a regular basis. We hoped church would be a place where we could find peace. Eventually I resented going to church because those other children talked about us all the time and we could hear them.

I became pregnant and had my first son at the age of fourteen. Due to being neglected by my mother, we ended up in foster care. I did not understand what foster care was at the time but I was grateful that I had somewhere to go. As a foster child, I did not understand who I was. I felt that I was not understood at times, and it seemed like everyone was against me. I expressed myself differently and my feelings came out that way. I was not perfect and sometimes I made mistakes. When I think of my foster mother and the social workers, I felt like they questioned if I could be loved. No one seemed to love me. I struggled with wanting to feel loved and giving my love in return. They questioned if I could be trusted. I had to convince myself I could trust them. They judged whether I could grow up and be somebody. After what I had been through, I was trying to convince myself that I was somebody and could be a good person. They judged whether or not I could succeed. I had to convince myself that I could be successful when all odds seemed to be against me. They evaluated if I could do well in school. I told myself I was doing well in school. When I realized that they did not know me, I fought to try to help them understand me. I guess I did not go about it the right way at times. They determined that I did not have a chance in life. I begged them to give me that chance or opportunity. I made mistakes and they questioned if I could be forgiven. I asked for forgiveness and the strength to forgive them. When they judged whether or not I could do it, I told myself I was doing it, just in my own way. When they seemed angry with me, I told them I was not perfect and did not want them to be upset.

They treated me like everything was my fault. I hoped that they realized I was not to blame. They acted like they would give up on me while I was trying not to give up on myself. When it seemed like they were letting me down, I struggled to not to let myself down. They acted like they had no patience with me, while I was trying to be patient with them and make them understand who I was. It was a constant battle with wanting them to understand me and how I felt about being judged and being compared to statistics. When I heard about the statistics that said I would raise my children on welfare, I cried about it, drew strength from it and proved statistics wrong.

While living with my foster mother, I had to attend church every Sunday. I did not understand what I was doing, but had to give myself to the Lord. My grandmother forced me to go to church in the summer. Then my foster mother did the same thing. I could not seem to get away from spirituality. Every Sunday service added more values and morals to my view on life. Things that I learned in Vacation Bible School gave me a better understanding. Crying out to God gave me comfort when I had no one else to turn to. Those were the times when I sat in church and started crying and could not stop.

After being in foster care for so long, I never developed a close relationship with my mother. The only time I heard about my mother was when she had been hurt. The realization of hearing about my mother being run over by a truck, or being in the hospital because she had been pistol-whipped was hard to imagine. Not being able to protect or help her was depressing at times. I wanted to retaliate against the person who caused her pain. I was helpless and did not know where she was most of the time. I do not know why I felt I needed to protect her from situations she put herself in but she never protected me.

While in foster care, I had two more children by two different men. I sought love and acceptance in these men and did whatever I thought I had to do, to make them desire me. I thought sex was the answer. My relationship with my foster mother was one of gratitude and frustration. She loved her children unconditionally and I understood that. When her children did something to my children or me, nothing was ever done about it. She promised to replace things and that things would change. That never happened. I did not fight to leave her house because I could not be separated from my children. When I saw my foster sister's children wearing my children's clothes, I just cried and remained silent. My foster sister even stole my money and jewelry. My foster mother promised to replace it all but never did. I cried about things I had no control over.

Having failed relationships with my children's fathers became a way of life for us. One of my relationships ended because my foster care placement was being disrupted, not to mention he was a manipulative and sneaky person. I was young and naive. The following two ended due to physical abuse and mental abuse. Those relationships helped me become the woman I am today. I love who I am and without those experiences I might have become a different person. Abuse changes a person for better or worse. I chose to get stronger after being abused.

The children and I lived with granddaddy for five years before I bought a home of our own. Momma came and went throughout the years while still using drugs. She eventually started stealing from us and my children saw their outfits and coats on the children down the street. They played with their own games and toys at their friend's house and initially did not know it. Momma still makes me cry to this day and most of the time I have a desire for her to be there for us. The children quickly learned what a drug addict was but I made sure they still gave her the utmost respect. I never had a choice about who my mother is any more than my children could choose their grandmother. In life there are some things we must accept, make the best of, and deal with while hopefully keeping our sanity in the process.

Eventually I outgrew the person who mentally abused me. After that, I was determined to stay in my own world with a few select friends. I desired to strive for a more meaningful and successful life for my children and myself. Since I was so young, I did not have much dating experience. My failed relationships made me stronger and convinced me to try harder at being successful. I mostly focused on my goals and did not pay attention to the issues that stressed me out. I worked two and three jobs, sometimes four, to support my children and me. I cried almost every night for the protection of my children and God's strength to see me through all my troubling times. Through most of my journey, I was also responsible for one of my nieces at one time or another.

> *"Develop success from failures. Discouragement and failure are two of the surest stepping stones to success."*

> **~Dale Carnegie**

When I failed or had a setback, I got through the hard times without once striking back at anyone who caused me pain. Every failed relationship and every hardship gave me more determination to do better. I found motivation by putting my thoughts on paper and crying every time I felt like it. I read motivational books, watched Oprah for inspiration, kept reading the bible, and saved inspiring e-mails. I refused to look at women in magazines, so I would not compare myself to them.

I refused to use drugs after having watched my mother's experience. I refused to use my traumatic experiences as an excuse to not succeed and I could not escape the feeling that something better was in the world for me. Society projected that I would raise my children on welfare assistance, and that they would grow up to be menaces to society because a single black woman could not raise boys on her own. It was also thought I would be a failure because I grew up in foster care and had four children before the age of twenty-one. I did not want to end up like my mother, and was determined to give my children a much better life than I had experienced. It was a fight to prove all the naysayers and the statistics wrong. I refused to let being a teen mother and being raised in foster care define or dictate my future. I remember when I gave birth to my third son. I could hear two nurses in the hallway talking about me while I lay in my hospital bed. My nurse was telling Nurse Wanda that she was getting ready to bring my baby to me. My nurse told Nurse Wanda I was only seventeen and this was my third child. Nurse Wanda wanted to know if my mother had been around. My nurse informed her that my mother did not supervise me. My nurse further told her that I was in foster care. Nurse Wanda stated, "Wow, this poor child does not have a chance in life." My nurse replied, "I know what you mean she should know better by now and ought to be ashamed of herself." Nurse Wanda said that children these days have no respect for themselves, and they just pop babies out left and right." My nurse told Nurse Wanda that this was my third child and that I was still in high school. She wondered how a child my age could have three children, and keep making the same mistakes. She thought it might be acceptable the first time, but three times was ridiculous. Nurse Wanda proceeded to say, "You know what they say about teen mothers and foster children, she'll be a statistic." My nurse told Nurse Wanda she was going to wake me up and bring my baby to me whether I was ready or not. I could not believe how they were talking about me since they knew nothing about my life or me. My nurse had not been very nice then I had to listen to her talk about me. She thought she had me all figured out. I felt hatred for her but quickly realized she did not have all the facts. Unfortunately, she thought I was like every other single teen mother without any goals in life. Looking around my cold room made me feel very alone. I knew my mother would never show up and Big Momma (my foster mother) would not visit me either. I hoped my baby's father would show up some time that day, and I guessed my caseworker would call or come by. I felt so confused and tried not to cry. I lay there waiting for my son to be brought to me. No one had told that it was official he would be going to my foster home with me. I felt like I had really messed up that time. I had not seen my caseworker since I had been admitted to the hospital. I started thinking he would not be able to come home with me and she was hesitant to tell me.

My thoughts were interrupted when my nurse entered the room. She gave me my baby and asked what was wrong with me. She said, "You are a mother again, so stop that crying. Everything is going to be alright." I told her I was fine and my stomach was hurting. She told me I would be fine in a few days, to get some rest and enjoy my baby. She was being too friendly. She told me to make sure I drank plenty of water so I would not become constipated. I thought to myself, she does not care. I did not have too much to say to my nurse and I wanted to call her the "B- Word." I lay there with tears in my eyes. I stared into my son's eyes trying to figure out what I would do if he could not come home with me. I had been threatened a million times about how hard it would be to place a teen mother with her children. I tried not to focus on what I heard the nurses say about me even though I had heard their entire conversation. They did not know anything about me but had my whole life figured out. They were very wrong and I was determined to prove to the world, my so-called friends that talked about me, my caseworker, most of all to my children and myself that I could succeed. I had to prove that I could be somebody. They were right, I was immature and irresponsible, but that did not mean I could not grow up and become somebody. I sat there crying about being seventeen with three children. I guessed it appeared to most people that I would not be able to grow up and be what society considered a pillar of any community. No one considered my unsupervised home life possibly contributed to my multiple pregnancies. I took total responsibility for what I had done, but adults should be held accountable for teenage pregnancy as well. I promised myself I would supervise my children as much as possible. I will forever be grateful that my foster mother allowed me to bring my third son to her home to live with us. We all have purpose in life and that was one of hers. Our life could have turned out very different had we'd been separated.

FAST: is an easy way to remember the sudden signs and symptoms of a stroke: Face dropping, Arm weakness, Speech difficulty, Time to call 911 ~ Additional signs of a stroke may include: Sudden numbness or weakness of the face, arm or leg, especially on one side of the body. Sudden confusion, trouble speaking or understanding. Sudden trouble seeing in one or both eyes. Sudden trouble walking, dizziness, lack of balance or coordination. Sudden severe headache with no known cause. about a third of people who experience TIA go ~on to have a stroke within a year.

It is hard to believe I suffered a TIA (Mini Stroke). Until years later, I never really dwelled on what it meant to have a stroke. I had to repeat the words over and over. One day my oldest son became serious when the topic came up. He asked a lot of questions and made a lot of statements. The first question was, "Don't people die from strokes?" Then he made the statement that people are left crippled or loses the ability to function at their normal capacity after having a stroke. After that, it hit me.

I started thinking about what happened to me when I had a stroke. I was in California to take the C-Best Exam and visiting a friend. I was talking on the phone when all of a sudden, the phone dropped out of my right hand. I tried picking it up but could not. I had to use my left hand since my whole upper right side was too weak. When I got back on the phone, I kept repeating, "What did you say?" After that, I could not remember the conversation and had no idea what my friend was talking about. Fortunately my niece was with me. I decided to return home to Las Vegas. My niece was a big help and navigated the entire trip with written instructions. The drive home was a total blur. Thankfully, we made it back safe. I took a nap and hoped I would be fine when I woke up. Some of the feeling returned on my upper right side when I got up. No one was around to communicate with to determine if my memory had returned. I woke up a second time to the sound of the telephone ringing. I remember asking the person on the phone several times what they were talking about. There was no doubt I had to go to the emergency room. After an overnight stay at the hospital, and a whole lot of tests, I was told I had suffered a stroke. Within two days my upper right side was fully functional and my memory was fine. Since I was much better, I chalked this incident up to being just another challenge I had to deal with. I did not focus on it or allow it to overwhelm me. I never carried myself like I had a stroke. After hearing about people my age and even younger who had died from what I had suffered, I thought about how serious my situation could have been. I was humbled at the thought and became more grateful for my life. With all that I had been through, having a stroke could have changed my life forever. I could not help but think about the possibility of my memory not returning or never regaining full use of my upper right side. At times I thought about people that died from having a stroke and people that never re-gained their memory or the feeling back in certain areas of their body. I thought about these issues but I did not become consumed with these ideas that might cause negative thoughts. Sure I had overcome the stroke, but so many people were not as fortunate. I wanted to believe that God decided to save me from what could have been a grave situation that might have changed my children's lives and me forever. There were times when I tried to figure out why my stroke did not have a tragic outcome. I quickly dismissed those thoughts and thanked God for giving me one more chance. I gave having a stroke no power. I did not allow the diagnosis to be my death sentence. I had moments when I thought about having the stroke and me surviving was a reminder that I have a greater purpose in this world.

2

THE BREAKING POINT

My relationship with Busta was the one I thought would last forever. I thought I had found my soul mate but instead I was left feeling very empty. I felt devastated when I realized we were never getting back together. I could not focus and I kept blaming myself for the break up, even though he had another woman. I felt defeated and did not feel good about myself. I was losing my self-esteem and felt very confused most of the time. I even wanted to blame God for allowing me to meet him. It felt like I was wrong for loving somebody. I started focusing on the negative things in my life and could not see anything good about my life after the break up. My head and heart were filled with negative thoughts and feelings that was making my attitude change.

I had survived being away from my mother while she was in prison, being sexually abused, being a teen mother, and being placed in foster care. I was a single parent; I had given birth to four babies, had endured physical and mental abuse, and had gotten through college all on my own. I thought for sure I could not handle any more milestones. I was frightened because I had already had a mini stroke while with Busta. I thought he would love me forever since I had been all I could be to him. The situation left me feeling uncertain about myself. I was a survivor but could not understand why this was happening to me. I wondered why Busta lied and played games. Thinking about him consumed my thoughts. My self-esteem began to waiver. I convinced myself that I was tired and ready to just give up and give in to "whatever" life had to offer. I foolishly convinced myself that I should accept whatever Busta had to offer just to have a man in my life. Being with him was an emotional roller coaster ride. I realized that I had a lesson to learn from that relationship and knew I had to move on. I was torn between wanting this man to be my soul mate and struggling with the reality of feeling like I was just another victim of his selfishness. He was responsible for more heartache than any other man. He came into my life after I had endured all that I had gone through. I was at peace with myself, and the direction my life was headed before we met. I could not figure out why God would allow a man to come into my life to lie to me, use me and then walk out of my life like I meant nothing to him. The reality of the relationship was lost in the fantasy of what was actually going on. He was a liar. Just as quick as he built me up, he brought me down. I went to seek therapy and talk about it, just to get through the day. I realized the purpose for going to therapy brought out so much more than a bad relationship. I had a very hard time accepting the end of our relationship. I still wanted to hang onto what I thought we had. I told myself I was the one that ended all the other relationships and could not understand why I was angry for having to end this one just to save my sanity. I was not ready to end it, even though I knew all the negative things about him. I felt like it was all fake and realized he never really wanted me in the first place. I started my own thoughts of self-destruction. That is what I get for telling myself those negative things, and tearing myself down. That was the wrong way of thinking and it took a long time to bring me back from the brink of destruction.

I did not give up when everything seemed hopeless, or contemplating suicide and turning against people. I did not make excuses for hating the world. I refused to become a victim of Busta's selfishness. I fought my way back to me, built the desire to do better, and continued to raise my sons to be self-reliant role models in society. I did not start using drugs or alcohol, I never prostituted myself and I did not blame anyone else but me. Being with him was my choice.

My spirituality, the tears I shed and writing helped get me through the relationship. I was determined to minimize the pain. Even though I had overcome a lot worse, at times I started to question myself as a woman and thought I could not make it without Busta. Foolish thinking about myself and I created those negative thoughts. I was left feeling empty at the thought of not having him in my life. Any of this sounds familiar or can you relate? Know that people serve a purpose in your life and once their purpose is clear move on.

> *"I've been stabbed in the back by those I need-ed most. I've been lied to by those I love. And I have felt alone when I couldn't afford to be. But at the end of the day I had to learn to be my own best friend because there's going to be days where no-one is going to be there for me but myself."*

~Wisdom quotes and stories

I thank God for the favor he showed me. I know I am blessed in spite of all I have been through. These experiences made me stronger. I had my weak moments when I felt like God was not there for me. I am not sure what I would have done without believing in God. Imagine if there was no religion, no purpose or nothing to believe in. If God had not been in my life, I would not have had anything to draw strength from, no one to cry out to and no reason to hope for change. Every time I started losing faith, I was reminded that my life had a greater purpose and a reason to see things through.

3

HOW TO RELEASE

I could not stop thinking about Busta today. He consumed my every thought. I woke up thinking about him and he was on my mind as I fell asleep. I imagined him attending meetings with me and us being the most powerful and influential couple in the world. I heard the bad and the good talk. We were the couple to be admired. I could not understand what went wrong since we were supposed to be together forever. Everybody thought we were the "cutest couple." I wondered what I had done or what I could have done differently. I desperately needed help and was determined to get over this situation so I could move on. After all, I did not want to be with someone who repeatedly treated me like something that needed to be scraped off the bottom of a shoe. I hoped I would be able to forget him and just move on. I wanted to let go.

I thought I was past drama in my life. I was tired and very disappointed because I thought after meeting Mr. Busta I would be happy for the rest of my life. It seemed I would snap if one more negative thing happened to me. I did not know what I would do if I had one more bad experience. Relationships play a significant part in how we feel. Moods are affected and can be responsible for our happiness or our emptiness. The choice is ours.

On the day of my first therapy appointment, I parked my car in front of the office building but took my time getting out. I contemplated turning around and heading back home. I was not sure what I would say and I did not know where to start. I had never seen a therapist and was not used to telling anyone about my problems except God. I figured what the heck, it was time to try something different. The therapist's office was in a secluded section of the building at the end of a hallway. I tried to relax while telling myself everything was going to be okay. I wondered what the doctor looked like and questioned if I was crazy for being there. A receptionist led me to Dr. Smith's office and I entered very slowly.

"Hello, my name is Dr. Smith, you may call me Rose. What is your name?"

"My name is Special."

"That is a very nice name. Is this your first time seeing a therapist?"

"Yes, I really do not know what to say."

"Let us talk about why you feel you need therapy, and take your time."

"I get angry easily, I am frustrated and very confused most of the time. A lot of things I am feeling are driving me crazy. I feel like I am about to lose my mind."

"Give me some examples of how you are feeling. I know you say you are angry, frustrated and confused but elaborate for me please."

"Well, one minute I feel like I have no problem helping people, the next minute I am angry for helping them. Why do I feel that way?"

"Is helping people making you angry and frustrated, or is it the people that you have helped that are making you feel this way? What people are you talking about?"

"I am talking about everybody that had bad intentions when they asked me for something. I am tired of feeling used after trying to be there for them. I hate feeling confused about how I want to respond and interact with them. I usually end up being hurt by people who are only looking out for themselves. They do not seem to consider my feelings."

"So you are saying people usually hurt you after you have helped them, is that correct?"

"Yes, that is all people have ever done. It is like being punished for caring about them."

"So why do you help people? Are they your responsibility?"

"I thought I liked helping people."

"You think you do not like helping people or would you have chosen different people to help?"

"It is not that I do not like helping people. The people I have helped usually end up hurting me, and every time I say I am not going to help anybody else besides my children, I go out of my way to help at all costs."

"Do you feel you have to help people? Are you responsible for them?"

"I do not know. Everyone depends on me but I do not have anyone to lean on when I need support. I hate to feel like my children only have me, but it is true, I am the only person they can depend on. I live in constant fear of letting them down. I hate disappointing the important people in my life. For instance, my family, the man in my life and my boss should not be let down. I just want my children to feel there will be someone else they can count on if they don't have me. Without asking, several people in my life know I will always be in their corner to give them the assistance they need. My children and me have never felt like we can depend on anybody. Somehow, it just does not seem fair."

"Sounds like you are developing a problem with trusting people."

"How can I have a problem with trusting when I give all I have without hesitation? I give physically, mentally and financially to other people all the time. I justify it by telling myself not to blame others for the way somebody else treats me. I usually let my guard down and in the long run I wish I had not."

"We need to work on your trust issues. I can tell you have a trusting nature and because you have trusted the wrong people you do not feel good about these situations. Would you like to talk about any other concerns?"

"I just got out of a relationship. I cannot seem to get over Busta. When I should be concentrating on my children or my job, he creeps into my thoughts. He is driving me crazy."

"How is he driving you crazy? Who is letting him drive you crazy, besides you? Did you just get out of the relationship or are you still in the relationship?"

"Both, if that makes any sense. This time I am going to stop seeing him forever. I refuse to let him back into my life. He is in my every thought. He is on my mind when I am drifting off to sleep and most mornings when I wake up. He is constantly on my mind."

"You sound like you are trying to convince yourself you are not going to see him again. He cannot consume you if you do not let him. He is not in control of you or your thoughts. You are allowing these thoughts to take over. What is wrong with thinking about him?"

"I want to hate him, but I can't."

"Why do you want to hate him? It is natural to love the worst person in the world. It is not that you do not love him, you do not like how he has made you feel."

"I feel like he used and manipulated me."

"Can you explain? How did he use and manipulate you?"

"Maybe I do not want to talk about him anymore. I cannot explain it."

"Nobody can make you feel anything you do not want to feel, Special, remember that. You are making yourself feel this way. You are constantly thinking about him. Nobody else is in control of your thoughts. You are the only one in charge of your every waking thought and your desires. No one can do anything to you without your permission. Do not give him that power over you. He did not take anything from you, you gave it to him."

"I did not let him do anything. He lied from day one and continued to lie throughout the entire relationship. I was wrong for trusting him. I told myself the relationship was too new to complain or say anything when I noticed things were not going as smoothly as I thought they should. I hoped against hope that eventually everything would change for the better once we got used to each other. As time went on, I realized I could no longer use my original excuse. The lies continued and became an everyday occurrence. Before I knew it, I had fallen in love, or thought I had and was convinced we were made for each other. I was sold on the idea and held onto that. He convinced himself that because I had never caught him in the act of cheating on me he had done nothing wrong. I was told over and over that he had never disrespected me and never would. I spent the rest of the time trying to figure out what I had done wrong. I thought the relationship could survive if I knew how to please him enough so he would not stray. I doubted myself and felt like a fool because a year later nothing had changed. While the sex got better, so did the lies. I refused to believe I was stressed out. Nothing felt right but it was hard to accept. I had bent over backwards thinking about the facts versus the fantasy. I was caught up in how I wanted the relationship to be and did not allow myself to see the truth. My self-esteem hit rock bottom and I did not have the energy to be the person I was before meeting Busta. I was caught up in the physical relationship and stayed because I did not want to be alone. I convinced myself that if I went along with things as they were and kept the peace, he would change."

"Do you still talk to him?"

"The relationship ended months ago. It seems like he calls when he gets bored. Busta thinks I still want to be with him. He says all the right things and I fall for it every time. I have rehearsed what I want to tell him about leaving me alone then I hear his voice and forget what I wanted to say. I get sucked in every time."

"So, are you saying he calls you? Why you do not call him and tell him how you are feeling?"

"I have done that a million times. He really does not care about how I am feeling. When I go off on him he does not pay me any attention. It goes in one ear and out the other. Usually when he calls I am feeling lonely and he talks about the way things were. He mentions how good we were in bed. Before I know it, he is knocking on my front door and we head straight for the bedroom. While basking in the afterglow, I start feeling like there is a chance we could make it work again. I start calling him but before long I realize nothing has changed and probably never will. Once I come to that realization I start feeling awful, I tell him I do not want to be a part of his games anymore. I tell him to leave me alone and not to call me anymore. I guess he ignores me. Eventually he calls and by then I am no longer angry. He waits long enough for me to calm down, sometimes weeks go by but eventually he calls."

"How long has this been going on?"

"Since we broke up! For some reason I cannot stay angry, and every time I convince myself it is over, I see again."

"I hope you realize this sounds like a pattern with him and patterns are not easy to break."

"Exactly, that is what I keep telling myself that I am tired of the pattern. I welcome him back one minute and the next I tell him to leave me alone. I convince myself how things could change for the better. Deep down inside I know I am only kidding myself. I know I deserve much better and need to move on since everything with him will probably remain the same."

"Since you feel this way, why do you still talk to him? Why do you give him this power over you? Is he forcing you to talk to him or to see him? Think about what you are saying. Or do you see him because you really want to? Be honest with yourself."

"I cannot explain it. I ask myself that all the time."

"I want you to think about that until I see you next week. I want you to put your thoughts on paper. Also think about other situations when you trusted someone and they hurt you or let you down. Go back as far as you can remember. Your name is Special for a reason. I bet you are a very special person. Start believing that."

"I can remember several situations when people let me down; hurt me, used, and abused me."

"What else is going on in your life? I know there are some positive things we can talk about."

"I have four wonderful young men. I am blessed because they are respectful, they got good grades in school, they are so handsome, and they make me proud. My boys are an exception to the rule. They do not fit the young black male teenage stereotype."

"Is that a smile I see? Life does not seem so frustrating when you talk about them. Your voice tone even changed. I know relationships are important in everybody's life but focus on the positive things. I hope you have something else going on in your life besides Busta and your children."

"I work two jobs that require me to work with people. I love people and I like both of my jobs."

"What do you do on these jobs? You must really like working with people for you to maintain two jobs where you must interact with them. How long have you been working two jobs?"

"I have been working with Family Services for over ten years. I answer the phone and take abuse or neglect referrals. I have been working at the casino for about a year. I like working with people, but at times I get frustrated. At the casino some people drink too much and they act like someone owes them something. Some of them seem to expect something for nothing."

"Your life sounds full Special. What do you do for yourself?"

"I get manicures and pedicures. On occasion, I go to the movies by myself."

"How did you feel about going to the movies alone?"

"At first I was apprehensive. Eventually I felt comfortable and really enjoyed myself. It turned out to be fun."

"Your life sounds normal to me. As things that bother you come to mind, I want you to start writing them down. Express your feelings as the thoughts occur. Next week, we will discuss these thoughts. I would like you to focus on more positive than negative thoughts."

"Thanks Dr. Smith, I needed to unload. It was great talking to you."

"Call me Rose, and sometimes when you say things out loud and hear yourself, it can have a new meaning for you. See you next week Special."

"Goodbye and thanks again Dr. Smith."

Out of respect I continued to call my therapist Dr. Smith.

Dr. Rose Smith is a very petite woman who walks with grace and style. She is in her mid to late thirties and looks much younger. She sits behind her desk and listens like she has two sets of ears while showing compassion at the right moment. She is a very classy dresser. She makes me feel relaxed but I cannot help but straighten up in her presence. She is very patient and made me feel comfortable enough to make me want to tell her about my whole life in one breath. Her office is very organized and the décor is coordinated. There is a fresh rosy candle scent in the air. I thought to myself I would like an office like that. Her smile lit up the room. She was so welcoming that I felt comfortable right away. Her focus was totally on me and she made me feel like I was her only patient. I wanted to talk to her forever about any and everything. This seems like a very good idea. There was no feeling of judgment.

> *"People come into your life for a reason, a season, or a lifetime. When you figure out which one it is, you will know what to do for each person."*

> ~ **Search Quotes**

4

LOVE ME OR LEAVE ME ALONE

Signs of Codependent Relationships: You enable your partner's unhealthy behaviors, and they enable yours. You minimize your needs and preferences. Instead of growing together, you deteriorate together. You feel increasingly bad about yourself. Your mood and self-respect are dictated by your partner's mood and behavior.
You feel devalued or disrespected by your partner. You feel frustrated or angry about how you're being treated but you don't speak up. Instead you "waffle between fight — getting into conflicts — or flight — keeping [your feelings to yourself]." You feel ashamed and embarrassed about what's really going on in your relationship.

I cannot believe how comfortable I felt while talking to Dr. Smith. I hope she did not think I was yelling at her. I have not thought about Busta as much as I used to. Sometimes I wish we had never met. After the last time I saw him I did not want anything to do with him. I was thoroughly fed up. Life was fun and games to him. He told me I had ruined the fun, we were having. He was having fun, but I was not. I tried to make him understand that my feelings were involved. He did not care. He was only thinking of ways to get me to have sex with him one more time.

I told him several times I did not want to see him anymore. He tried to push the issue and acted like it was a big deal to see me. The more I said no, the more he acted like he really wanted to see me. The conversation went from me saying, "No I am not messing around with you anymore", to "Let's just talk." Then it became, "I will meet you at the corner store just to see you. I just want to talk to you." That was a lie and a set up, and I fell for it again.

After telling Busta no, over and over again, he still insisted. I told him I would meet him at the store after I got out of the shower. I called and told him I changed-my mind. He still insisted. The next thing I knew he was in front of the house. I convinced myself that it would be no big deal to see him and get it over with. I continued telling him no. He kept insisting that he had to see me. I was being strong, still saying no, but my body was saying, "Go ahead, it's cool." I told myself since I was not seeing anybody else it did not matter.

I went outside and joined him in his car. We laughed and talked a little bit. It felt like old times. I had to admit I was glad to see him. He wanted to talk about our sex life. I knew where that conversation was headed. A tug-of-war started between my heart and my body. I remained strong and told him "no" as I was getting out of the car. He followed me to the front door. I knew I was in trouble. Before I knew it, we were in the bedroom. I desperately tried to resist when the touching started. I told myself, just get it over with; he is not going to give up. I stopped resisting. Yes, I gave in one more time. It seemed like old times until I opened my eyes. When I looked at him, I was disappointed, mostly with myself. All of a sudden in my eyes, he was not the old Busta. I knew this was the end. Those old feelings were no longer there. I hated myself for breaking all my rules and lowering my standards for him. Basically I felt stupid for the way he made me feel. I knew then that it was definitely over. I realized I deserved much better. He realized something was wrong. It finally dawned on him that I was not responding to him, that I was not my usual self. On a regular day sex with him would be wild and full of passion. Not today, I did not want any passion and I knew what was going to happen once he was satisfied. I could not do it. Tears filled my eyes at that thought. He noticed and had the nerve to get mad. I knew I could never cry in front of him again. I would not do it. I was tired and fed up. I could not pretend it was no big deal anymore. I knew he would not call me for days. I imagined if he did call the conversation would not be the same. I knew I would spend time wondering who he was calling and spending time with since we were not together. My mind was racing a thousand miles a minute. He wanted to continue while I lay there trying to pretend everything was okay. He got mad and told me to stop faking. He thought we were having fun. He wanted me to respond but I could not. I tried to tell him I had said no but he was not listening. He was only thinking about what he wanted, and did not care about me or my feelings. I asked him if he cared about me at all. He told me to call my friend and tell her how I had just treated him. He down played the whole situation and acted like it was no big deal. He got dressed and started to leave. I was so angry that tears filled my eyes once again. He just looked at me like I was crazy and left. I listened for the door to close just waiting for him to leave. I lost it, and began crying uncontrollably. I could not believe how insensitive that idiot had been. I was so angry for being in the same situation one more time. I felt so worthless and used. I called him to give him a piece of my mind. When he answered the phone, I had nothing to say. I just said, "I will talk to you later." In his happy go lucky, I do not care that you are upset, forget your feelings tone, he said, "Make sure you call me tomorrow, okay?" I just hung up. I knew neither of us would be making that call.

I wish I could have taken that day back. The situation was not good. I swore, if he called I would not answer. I wondered why I was wasting my time. He did not have a job, had no sense of responsibility, he was not dependable, and was living with another woman. I hated my situation with him and wanted to forget him once and for all. I should have listened to Ashanti's, "It's Over Baby," Jill Scotts, "Run Across My Mind," and J Lo's "I'm Gone." or Mya's, "I'm Moving On." I deserved to be treated a whole lot better.

Determined to think about something more pleasant, I wondered what my friend Mercedes was doing. I needed to talk to her. We met during my college years. She was in her late twenties, and had a unique look. Even without make-up, she looked like a supermodel. She was working toward her degree and owned her own home. She does not have any children. Her remarkable personality attracted the right people. We have known each other for more ten years.

During that time we developed a relationship built on our ability to share our life experiences with each other, keeping each other's secrets, and trying to support each other the best way we knew how. We argued, as most friends do and sometimes threatened to end our friendship. We would fuss and cry, but in the end, our friendship got stronger as the years passed. Our friendship required patience just like any other relationship. I decided to call her.

"What's up Mercedes?"

"What's up Sweetie?"

"I know we agreed to stop talking about sorry men, but I saw a therapist today and I talked about Busta."

"Why? That is your problem? You are always talking about him."

"Well, the conversation started going in one direction, and then I ended up talking about him. I got mad while talking to her. He had the nerve to call me after the last time I saw him."

"What did he say? I know there was a part of you that was glad he called. I am the same way when Koby calls, when I am angry with him."

"I did not answer the phone. He left a message asking me to call him. He sounded like everything was cool. I do not see the purpose, things are not going to change, and I really do not feel like I have anything to say to him. You cannot teach old dogs new tricks, right? Besides I have been telling Busta about himself for a long time. If I did not have anything going for myself I would end his life. Just kidding."

"Girl, Busta is not stupid, he seeks out women like you. Women who have things going for themselves, and he knows you are not going to throw all your accomplishments away for him. If you were some twobit tramp with nothing to lose you probably would want to see him hurt. I do not know why these men think we are going to keep letting them use and abuse us. One day they will meet that one woman that will put an end to their games."

"It is all good, because Alicia Keys' song "Karma" and Angie Stone's song " Karma" are two examples of how it will catch up with them. Men think that things will continue on an even keel. What they do not realize is we eventually reap what we sew. Pay back is usually two or three time worse than anything done in the past. That is another reason I really need to get away from him. I do not want to be around when the stuff hits the fan. So, what has been going on with you?"

"Working on school assignments, my internship, doing a lot of reading, and trying to maintain a work-out schedule. Did I tell you that fool Koby's been calling me? I refuse to answer the phone when he calls. He did leave a message asking if I wanted to go shopping for clothes. I might have to answer the next time if he keeps offering to buy Louis Vuitton and Bebe. He is so full of himself. He thinks he can throw something I like in my face, and I will come back to him. Once they spend time with us and spend some money they take a break and do not call for weeks. When they do call, they act like nothing has changed, and that it was no big deal that they ignored us. They want us to think we are the "one", and act like everything is cool."

"Girl, we both know it is part of the game. If any man calls a woman offering to buy Bebe outfits he will get back on her good side."

"Exactly, it is a game, until they get you all caught up in the intimacy and shopping for you. They just need to feel confident that they still have you."

"There will be a woman who will get him caught up in something he cannot get out of, or she might dog him out and treat him like she was treated."

"That is what I am talking about."

"Let's see how the game goes. The man and woman meet and fall in love. The woman starts catching him in lies. She tries to be cool with it and tells herself it is all in her head. She plays mind games with herself while trying to make sense of the lies and the cheating. She is in denial and tries to figure out what went wrong. She blames herself and begins to question her qualities and attributes as a woman. She knew she was too good to him, but still blames herself for his behavior. She breaks it off, but he catches her when she is feeling lonely and convinces her to take him back, but they never really get back together. After about six months she realizes that she was just sleeping with him and they were never back in a relationship. She thinks about all the positive things, and the reasons they were so good together. He wants to reminisce about good times and mostly about the physical part of their relationship. He sets her up, gets her back in bed and the cycle starts all over again. Her loyalty makes her stay in what she thinks is a committed relationship and she will not see or date anyone else. She knows she deserves better but loneliness gets the best of her. She knows she loves him, and convinces herself that if she just hangs in there, things might change. After a while, a lot of wasted time has gone by and everything remains the same. His lies and manipulation work until she gets fed up and decides enough is enough."

"Girl, you are so right."

"I am irritated, I will call you tomorrow."

I knew Mercedes was right when she said all I do is talk and think about Busta. I needed to focus on something else. I have so many important issues in my life. I started thinking about what to say to him the next time he called. When he calls I never say what I rehearse because I get so caught up with hearing his voice and be so glad he called. I make myself feel depressed until he calls again. I would perk up the minute I heard his voice. Most of the time I would be feeling very irritated. Little things ticked me off, and I got extremely angry over little or nothing. If I had not been working, I probably would have sat at home and cried all day. Knowing he is not that important.

5

MOVING ON

As usual, I was lost in my thoughts. At times I thought about Busta. I knew I should not start my day with Busta on the brain. It was time to leave home and drop Chris off at school before heading to work; I did not want to be late. I started yelling at Chris for no reason other than the irritation with myself. Thoughts of Busta were creeping in my mind. Over and over I told myself to leave him alone because he was not worth the heartache or the trouble. I would tell myself not to be rude and return his call because I hated it when my calls were not returned. Oh, but that was just the excuse I wanted to use to justify calling him. It seemed okay to just leave a message again about leaving me alone, that this is the last phone call and insist on him not calling me again.

"Hold on Chris, here I come." I blocked the number first so he would not know I was calling. (Beep)

"Hello Busta, (hoping I sounded rational), I got your message the other day. You know I think it is rude when people do not return calls. I just wanted to tell you I got your message and I do not need people like you in my life. I want a person that treats me like the lady I am. I need somebody that works and is responsible. Oh, and you need to grow up. Like I have said before, your son sees me as a good woman. If he notices that I put up with your lies and manipulation he will probably think it is okay to treat women the way you do. No matter what you tell him, he knows what he sees. Call me when you get a job and are doing something positive with your life. You need to settle down and get a grip on reality and take responsibility for your actions. Do the right things in your life. We both know you are better than what you have become. Do not call me, because I will not be calling you."

I hope that would do it. Oh that felt good, that should stop him from calling. I hope I did not sound stupid. All day while I was at work, that message was on my mind and I repeated what I said back in my mind over and over. I thought about what I should have added. I noticed I had missed his call. I could not believe after leaving that message this morning that still did not stop that idiot from calling. He is playing games. Trying to see what mood I am in and how I am going to respond to him. He needs to grow up. One of his other women will really hurt him one day. I have contemplated too many scenarios on how to get back at him for messing with my feelings. Enough of that, time to get back to work.

I started thinking about my friend Alexis. She is one the most levelheaded people I know. She is very short and her feet look no bigger than her five-year-old son's. She has that light skin, long hair thing going on and on a rainy day she might be in a pair of high-heeled sandals. She has her Master's Degree in Psychology, she owns her own home and her Lexus is paid for. Unfortunately, she has "baby daddy" drama. She is smart though; she refuses to let him back into her life. We met each other at the gym. During our first conversation we discovered we had worked for the same agency. We developed a workout schedule that we both try to stick to. Our friendship grew from loving the same type of work and realizing we drew strength from each other's positive attitudes. Most of our conversations were about developing a business plan, promoting a new idea or just ways to improve our financial status. She understood when I talked about Busta. She never passed judgment or told me how to handle my relationship with him. I should have focused on the business and positive parts of our conversations and left Busta out of them. I realized through her relationship with her son's father the drama I did not go through with my children's fathers. I also realized just how much men can be so irresponsible when it comes to their children. I have worked so much and have been able to provide for my children on my own, that I fail to see just how much I was doing on my own.

Alexis had not showed up at the gym. I called to make sure everything was okay.

"Special is that you?"

"Yes, Alexis it is me, what is up? Why weren't you at the gym today? I am leaving the gym now, heading to my car."

"I did not make it to the gym because I was up all night explaining to my baby's daddy it is over. Let me tell you what Michael did. He has this new dance that is too funny. He has a song to go along with it. I do not know where he learns this new stuff he comes up with. I do not play these songs in my house. I definitely do not dance like that; maybe he hears it on the radio."

"That sounds cute. I love the relationship you have with your son. A person cannot talk to you without hearing about Michael, which is tight. You make me wish my boys were still five or younger."

"Right now it is all about Michael and me. Did I tell you his daddy had the nerve to call and ask if he could come home? Is he crazy or what? He has not done anything different since he left almost year ago. He did not send me a dime the whole time he was gone. How can a brotha think they can keep their money to themselves while all of ours is spent on our children? What is up with that? I have daycare, sports activities, juice boxes, coats, and clothes to buy. Not to mention everything he sees in the toy isle of the stores. The new cartoons and the action figures are getting out of control. His Dad gets to spend all his money on himself. Let him tell it, I would be wrong for taking him to court and request child support."

"I hear you. I get tired of talking about men. Which reminds me; I got another hang up call today from a blocked number. It was probably one of Busta's women. I refuse to hate her; she has not done anything to me."

"I remember when you got the first call. That is cool you feel that way because she more than likely has no idea what your relationship is with Busta. Some women spend so much time blaming and getting mad at the other woman. It is the men that are dogging us and causing us to feel bad. Not the other woman"

"Yeah, I know, right?"

"I cannot imagine calling another woman, for what? You never know what the man has told her."

"You are right and women need to consider that before blaming the other woman. The girl had the nerve to tell me that I knew Busta has a woman and to leave him alone. Then she said I must have no self-esteem because I'm messing with a man that is in a relationship. Busta never told me he was in a relationship in the beginning. My intuition led me to the truth. I am glad I had enough sense to pay attention, just not before I call myself falling in love"

"It is not your responsibility to play private investigator to determine if what he says it true. It is sad we have to deal with lying men. We are screwed from the beginning because we trust them and believe their lies from day one."

"Well, I told her she must be the one with low self-esteem. She is calling another woman, she knows her man is cheating on her, and she stays with him. She better be glad I am not a hater. I could have said some things that would mess with her mind. I will never disrespect another woman because of a cheating man. It does not make me the better woman or a better person."

"Women need to think first. Calling another woman is not the answer. We should stop trying to please these men and insist they get their act together. It would be to our benefit if we got together and had decent conversations to get to the truth. The men need to be confronted more or the drama will never end. More than likely both are being played. Some men set the situation up like that. Once their woman finds out they are cheating, the females start hating on each other and blaming the other woman, thinking she knew he had a girlfriend. The men act like her friend knew the girlfriend and had something to do with it too. It is only to make them not speak to each other and confront him. They play up to the scenario that her friends are starting trouble, and convince their woman that her friend wants him too. So nobody is talking and every woman is mad at the other. It is hard to get caught if nobody is talking to each other."

"I know. We want to blame the other woman and have an attitude with her, when it is really the man who is lying, conniving, and manipulating us. It is sad how we allow them to use us as women."

"Women need to learn to stick together and realize that some men are who they are and no matter how good we are to them. The finest, the most educated, and the richest woman with the best sex in the world cannot change a DOGG until he is ready."

"Girl, you are crazy, but you know, you are right."

"Girl, you hear Michael? He loves this song and swears he can sing. I will call you back when I get him settled down."

"Okay talk to you later."

6

ACCEPTING CHILD'S
FATHER DEATH

On my way to pick up Chris before going to my second job, I remembered telling Dr. Smith how frustrated I was at times since I had to work with customers in the casino who sometimes drank too much and expected something for nothing. Fortunately, I do have some customers who make my day. Those are the ones I look forward to seeing and made going to my second job easier. I drove to my son Chris' school to pick him up and hoped he would be waiting and ready to leave. Chris hit me with questions as soon as he got in the car. As a mother you can only hope and pray that you raise your son or sons to be decent, strong, and independent. I was doing the best I could on my own.

"Momma you go to your second job tonight?" "Yes, Chris what is up? Why are you asking?" "We need another car, bad. You have to leave work, pick me up, I drop you off at your other job, then I go pick up Donte' and his friends from school. I have to drop Donte's friends off at home and then we get something to eat and head home. That is a lot of driving momma. It takes forever with all the traffic. Your car is going to start falling apart in a minute."

"I know Chris; it is just easier this way. At least I do not have to worry about how you and Donte' are getting home. Before you started driving, people probably stopped answering their phones thinking one of you were going to ask for a ride. I got tired of wondering how the two of you were getting home. I hate putting that responsible on you. I hope you are not getting frustrated because you have to leave basketball practice early."

"That's okay, it's cool momma, and we do what we have to do. Since Patrick is away at college, we are all we have right now. My coaches have been making negative comments. I just shrug it off and deal with it. It is gonna be okay Momma; we are going to be all right. Things will get better and I hope I make it to the NBA."

"You are so sweet Chris, I hope you make it too, you play basketball so well."

"Momma, I am getting tired of Donte' getting in the car acting crazy. If he is not complaining about my driving, he is messing with the radio, or it is always something when I pick him up. I think he acts stupid to show off in front of his friends."

"He don't mean no harm Chris, pay him no mind and do not let him get you upset."

"I know Momma but it gets on my nerves, it is always something. He complains about my driving or he is switching the radio stations and he is constantly telling me which way to go. I want to, but I never remind him that he needs to get his driving license and he has the nerve to tell me how to drive."

"He will get his license soon. Then he will see how it feels to do all the driving. When was the last time you talked to Patrick?"

I have not talked to him in couple of days. Guess I should call him. The last time we talked I was supposed to call him back after I did my homework, but I forgot."

"I talked to him last night. He did not sound too happy. I do not think he is doing well in school this quarter. I think he is distracted and not concentrating."

"He is alright Momma. It's been hard but I bet my GPA is a 4.0 this time, I can just feel it. I told you momma I am going to make you proud of me. I've learned that I can get good grades if really apply myself. I used to blame it on the teacher's on purpose. I just wish my daddy was here to see what a good student I am and how well I am playing basketball."

"It is okay Chris, he knows. I wish he was here to see how well you are doing too."

"I just know my life would be different if he was still alive. I would definitely have my own car. I am glad he taught me how to drive before he died. He was the greatest father a kid could have. He made it to all my basketball games and videotaped every one of them. He did all the driving. That was something you never had to worry about and I hate that you have to worry about it now. I realize how he made things easier for you."

"I know Chris. He did make things easier for me when it came to your needs. A lot of father's do not realize that helping with the little things makes the mother's life much easier. Some men seem to think they are expected to buy expensive clothes and gadgets all the time. That is not always the case. Taking responsibilities is not just buying the child stuff. I am glad you still hold on to memories of your Dad and how important he was in your life. I remember him saying he would make sure you had a car. He was a good father. Let's hope you do not have the medical problems he had."

"I miss him so much momma. Most nights I cry myself to sleep while imagining how different things could be if he was still around."

I leaned over to give Chris a peck on the cheek and told him I loved him as he parked the car to let me out at the casino.

"Boy momma, this traffic is too bad. It will take forever to pick up Donte'."

"Just take your time Chris. I get off at midnight, be outside when I walk out that door, okay?"

"Yes momma, I love you too"

I finally broke down four months after Big Chris' death. I was being strong for my son, and had done a good job until then. I even spoke at the funeral without crying. One day I got a call from the school telling me I needed to speak to the dean about Chris. Without thinking, I automatically told the secretary she needed to call his father. There was a long silence until I realized she could not call him because he was dead. I told her I would be there as soon as I could. I asked my supervisor if I could leave early. She knew I arranged for Big Chris to be available while I was working, but things had changed. Before I made it around the corner, reality kicked in. I cried uncontrollably and asked God why He had taken Big Chris way before his time. God knew I needed him to be there for his son. I asked God over and over again why he had to be the father that died, why him? I did not realize just how much of the little things he did that made a big difference in my daily routine. He made my life so much easier since I did not have to worry about Lil Chris and his needs. Since he was unable to work and could not help much financially Big Chris made up for it in a lot of other ways. If only other father's would see it that way. He made my life easier just knowing he would be at all of Chris' games when I couldn't make it. He was able to shop for him and did all the driving I could not do while working. I did not know how to buy Little Chris a suit for the funeral because Big Chris bought all of his dress clothes and shoes. I had to call Big Chris' best friend for some help. I slowed down while driving. I did not know where the emotions came from. I was angry because I had to leave work early and meet with the dean since I was not used to going to the school about Lil Chris' issues. His dad always handled everything.

I met Big Chris my sophomore year at Valley High School. We lived in the same neighborhood and one day he sent his friend to ask for my phone number. We started a relationship after that and I had Lil Chris doing one of things I thought I had to do to make a guy like me and be with me. He helped me get to school so I wouldn't have to take the bus and gave me lunch money. He was a good father.

Lil Chris is my sweetheart baby. He is very attentive and still kisses me good night. I hope he does not have heart problems or develop diabetes, like his father. He has a heart of gold and always seems to know when I need uplifting words. He is very trusting and has a pure and free heart. He wants to move all his friends in with him, because he wants to make sure everybody is all right. He is very close to his oldest brother Patrick. Chris is younger than his brother Donte' and they seem to compete with each other all the time. Chris is very handsome, makes everyone laugh and the girls love him. He can turn a bad situation into something comical.

7

MOMMA'S WAY OF COPING

Addiction: Nature or nurture? Studies have shown that both genetic predispositions and environmental causes are factors that equally contribute to the development of alcoholism and drug addiction within the family system. More than 28 million Americans are children of alcoholics, and nearly 11 million are under the age of eighteen. For children of parents addicted to drugs or alcohol, life can be a nightmare riddled with confusion, fear, anger, and resentment. Alcoholism and drug addiction tend to run in families; children of addicted parents are more at risk for alcoholism and other drug abuse than are other children. Additionally, the use of substances by parents and their adolescent children is strongly correlated; generally speaking, if parents take drugs, sooner or later their children will take drugs too.

I like my job, but anything goes when you work with people at the Casino. I was in the employee dining room with a headache because I was thinking too hard. I was not sure I could handle Dr. Smith's request. She wanted me to think and write about people that hurt me. She has no idea how many issues I have. I will be writing forever. This time my mind is not on Busta. My drug-addicted mother has been on my mind the past few days. Drugs have been my mother's way of coping. I wonder if she will ever get off drugs and be free of her demons. Momma will never admit she was wrong for what she put my sisters and me through. A child is not supposed to worry if their mother will come home, or where their next meal will come from. We worried all the time about our mother. I will never forget the things she did; like leaving us at home alone for days at time. The last time my mother left us alone my sister Precious was taken from school and placed in Children's House, the safe haven for neglected and abused children. Momma had been gone for three days and no one knew where she was. She told us she was going to pick up the food stamps. She did not want us to go with her and said she would be right back with groceries. A few days later a friend told me she saw her walking down Jackson Street late one night. I tried not to worry about her. The social worker came to check on us twice while momma was away. I hoped she was all right. When she returned early one morning she looked very tired and her blouse was ripped. She told me someone had beaten her, knocked her down and took the food stamps. All I could do was stare at her. She did not mention how we were going to eat that night or how we were going to get food. She just went to bed and slept the whole day.

Our dirty clothes were piling up and we needed to wash the few clothes we had. I wondered how many people noticed we had to wear the same clothes over and over again. When momma finally woke up she left us alone again without even saying goodbye. We were left alone most to the time. I wanted to know what she was doing, where she was going and whom she was with. I could not figure out why she kept leaving us. I thought we had done something to make her angry. We always kept the house clean but maybe we did not do it right. If we had done something to her we could not figure out what it was. I tried to think of a positive reason for her leaving us again. Since we had not eaten in a few days I hoped she had gone to get us something to eat. We waited all day for her to return. I cried and prayed to God that she was all right since she was gone most of the day. My sisters finally went with their friends so I knew they were okay. I walked across the street to my aunt's house to ask for something to eat but she was not home either.

I went to my friend's house down the street. She was eating Top Ramen Noodles and offered me a pack. She let me cook and eat at her house. When I was almost finished eating, I noticed she was staring at my noodles. She told me they were not fully cooked. I did not know what she meant. My noodles were white and I thought that was how they were supposed to be cooked. She told me if they were still white they were not done. I felt so stupid and wondered if I had been eating them partially cooked all along. How was I supposed to know, I was only a child.

I still could not find my mother and nobody in the neighborhood had seen her. I went my Auntie's house, she was not home either and my cousins were home alone. Much later that day my mother finally showed up. She looked like her mind was somewhere else; she just stared into space. I kept asking her questions and she just looked at me like I was speaking another language. She never answered my questions and I could tell she was getting very irritated. Momma staggered around the house from room to room. She could not keep still. I went to my God Sister's house to baby-sit her child. I could not find my sisters anywhere; they were supposed to be right down the street. I hoped they were nearby and were okay. I vowed to myself I would never leave my children home alone and they would never go hungry.

I spent most of my weekends baby-sitting at my God Sister's house while she went out with her friend's. I hoped to make some money but she often failed to pay me and made promises she did not keep. I got a lot of handed down clothes and shoes from her that were too big. I accepted the clothes and shoes anyway just so I could have something different to wear. Week after week I convinced myself that eventually she would pay me, but she never did. I was young and believed the things she promised me and hoped that she would make good on her word. I loved her son anyway, so I did not mind watching him. When I returned home, the house was always empty. I usually had to search for my younger sister, Precious. She spent most of her time running around with her friends. My mother would show up hours later looking for something to eat or fussing about something. She always looked so tired and worn out. I had no idea what she had been doing, or who she had been with. She rarely talked to me and I always walked away with tears in my eyes. I started thinking about things she had done in the past. I thought about the day momma was sitting outside on the wall in front of the apartments. She was frozen in one spot with slobber running down her chin. My younger sister and I were looking out the window and were afraid to go outside because momma was not moving. We had no idea what was wrong with her. Our friends came around and they were staring, pointing at her and laughing. They knocked on the door and asked us to come get our mother. We did not know what to do. A man who was walking down the street stopped to see what was wrong with her since she was not moving. He picked her up and brought her inside the house. He put a glass of water up to her mouth and she suddenly moved. My sister and I cried because we were so scared. The man left once he thought momma would be all right. We still did not know what to do. She was high on drugs and there was nothing for us to do but cry for her.

The children outside were telling each other my mother was high on a drug called Sherm. I hated them for talking about her, but all I could do was cry and listen to them while they made fun of my momma. I wondered why she would embarrass us like that. I could not figure out why she continued to do those things and often wondered what was wrong with her. I told myself that when I grew up and had my own children, I would never put them through the things I went through. I would never embarrass them like that. She would not even look at my sisters and me. She had nothing to say for herself and we still did not know what to do. We were too embarrassed to go outside. Momma just went to her bedroom and shut the door. Precious and I knew the drill. Later she would sneak away when she thought we were not looking. We always heard her leave. She continued to leave us home alone for hours or days at a time. There was never any food in the house so we had to make do with eating sugar or syrup on a piece of stale bread. There was never anything left over in the refrigerator from another meal. It did not help that we never knew where our big sister was. I was so frustrated and angry; again all I could do was cry. Momma was wrong for the things she put us through. Eventually we were placed in foster care because of momma's drug addiction. We were sure her drugs were more important than we were. That made me feel awful and we hoped it was not our fault.

Precious, my younger sister and I were together most of the time. She became the party animal in the family. She would go out every night if she could; she acted irresponsible at times but would always bounce back one way or the other. Precious loves to be the center of attention so she always looks her best and buys the newest fashions to fit every occasion. Some way or another, the bills usually get paid. She knows everybody and always tries to keep the peace. She is a strong willed woman, just do not cross her or there will be hell to pay. Precious will not straight up start any trouble, but she has no problem ending it. She escapes life and the things that has happened to us by partying. I think she entertains herself so she does not have to think about all the heartache. I deal with her frustrations and take care of what she does not. I have become her momma figure and I just carry the weight of what she cannot handle. She has five children and I usually handle most of their needs financially.

My older sister is Dimples, she does things her own way, but will make an appearance at the right time. She is very petite and always looks attractive with the cutest hairstyles that she does herself. She has the prettiest light brown eyes and can be a bad girl with a temper who will fight if you cross the line. She will not hold back no matter who you are. She has a good side and a mean side. Just like Momma, Dimples has three girls. I constantly cry and pray that God watches over them. It hurts that I could not take them all in at once, to protect them from the world.

The phone rings, while looking through my purse for it I wondered who it could be. It is Precious.

"What is up Precious, where are you? Please tell me you are at work."

"Yes Special, I am at work but I am on my break right now. How about you, are you at work?"

"Yeah, I am on break too. I saw a therapist today."

"What did you do that for? Hell, I can tell you a thang or two. What? You on that Busta trip again? I told you to forget him. Watch what I tell you, when you finally get over him you are going be trying to figure out what was the big deal anyway, and then you will realize he ain't 'bout nothin'. Then you are going to get mad because you wasted too much time and energy on him. Watch what I tell you, you will see. I went through that drama too many times and when I finally got over it, I realized it was nothin' to sweat about."

"Anyway, have you heard anything about momma?"

"No, and I am not sure if I want to. You know she has nine lives and has used up at least seven of them. The last time we heard something about her she was pistol whipped until she was unconscious. Her teeth were busted out, she could not eat and her eyes were swollen shut. Before that happened, people were calling and asking if we heard she was found dead. Before that she got hit by a car, would you like me to continue? We have not heard anything because she is probably in jail this week. At least as long as she is in jail we do not have to worry about her."

"I guess you are right. My therapist made me think about a lot of things in my life."

"Well you go right ahead. A therapist cannot tell me anything. If I have financial problems, she is not going to give me any money, and she makes more money than I do. I need the money to pay her to fix my financial problems. I do not think so! I guess you got to do whatever it takes to get over Busta. I can get over my drama without a therapist."

"That is you! Besides it is better to talk to someone who is not personally involved. I wish I could just say forget him. I do not know what the big deal is either. I do not expect my therapist to fix it, but it was good that I could unload on her. She just listened without interjecting. I am worried about momma though. The last time she went to jail she wrote letters that made me cry. And as usual, she got out and did the same old thing. She has been in the streets for over twenty years, when will she learn?"

"You know I do not let what momma does get me upset any more. No matter what anybody says, she is going to do, what she wants to do. It is her decision to be in the streets. Granddaddy lets her return to his house every time. Momma will not stress me out. After she stole from you and your kids, you let her back in the house too. She will be all right. God is keeping her out there for a reason. Eventually, something will happen whether good or bad. I hope for the good, but I hope she is in jail and they keep her this time."

"I hope she is in jail too. She just worries me and every time she goes to jail she act like she is going to change. She gets out and goes right back out there in them streets. Will she ever change?"

"Girl, stop worrying about momma. She will be all right. She got about three lives left. LOL"

"Girl you are crazy, you would make me laugh. Let me get back to work."

"Remember what I said; forget Busta and your therapist. It is Busta's loss. Think about what you are losing and what he lost. Do not talk to me anymore about this drama. I am supposed to unload on you about my issues not the other way around. Love ya sis."

"Yeah, yeah, yeah, love you too."

8

NEVER TOO EARLY TO TELL

Just when I thought all the drama was over when it came to a man I met Tyree. I hoped he would never call me again. I refused to deal with another person that tried to put pressure on me and make me feel some type of way. I thought I had learned my lesson for good after putting my relationship with Busta behind me. Tyree is a brotha I met while changing the flat on my car. Yes, I know how to change a tire. He seemed cool so I gave him my real phone number. He has a light skinned complexion, he is tall, has a baldhead, and he is employed. He was headed to work when he took over and changed the tire for me. Cool, I thought to myself, this man is up at 6 A. M. in a work truck, and he is not afraid to get dirty. He said he lived by himself and that was quite impressive. I wondered why he was single. It did not take long for me to find out. Tyree had more issues than I care to count.

My phone rang at 12:30 A. M. I had just gotten home from work and wondered who would be calling this late. I thought twice before answering.

"Hello!"

"Special, what's up? This Tyree, why haven't I heard from you? Are you ignoring my calls?"

"Excuse me, why are you talking to me like that and why are you calling so late?"

"I haven't heard from you in two or three days. I know you just got off work, what's up with that?"

"I am busy, did you forget I work two jobs? We just met and we do not talk on a daily basis."

"Why can't we? If you really wanted to talk to me you would."

"Anyway, what's up?"

"Are you brushing me off? I was trying to see what's up with you, but I see you are too busy for a brotha."

"Do not take it like that, between my children and my jobs I do not have much time for anything or any-one else."

"When I helped you fix that tire you had time to talk. I guess you felt obligated to give me your number. I've only talked to you a few times since then."

"No I did not feel obligated, I thought you were cool and I appreciated what you did for me. I did tell you I work a lot and I know I told you I have four children."

"Yeah but two of them don't even live with you."

"What? You think they are not a priority because they do not live with me. Do you really think I am not responsible for them because we are not under the same roof?"

"No. I'm not saying that, but you know what I mean."

"No, I do not know what you mean. I spend half my time working and the other half either on the phone with my children or running errands with and for them. I guess you feel you would not have to be responsible for your children if they did not live with you! Am I right? It sounds like you feel free as a bird and not care or want to spend time with them as much as you could. My children will always be a priority no matter what!"

"Well, I don't feel that way. I'm just sayin'."

"Well, it is late and I need to get in the shower."

"What? You're finished talking to me? I'm not ready to get off the phone. Let me take you to get something to eat tomorrow. We can go get some lobster or go any place you like. I've been trying to spend time with you but you keep putting me off."

"Let me call you tomorrow, I need to see what my sons are doing."

"Yeah right, just tell a brotha anything. I just want to take you to eat, so you can chill out and relax, no strings attached."

"One of my boys plays football and the other will be playing basketball soon. I need to see what their schedules look like."

"Whatever, call me when you get a chance. I don't have time to be put off anymore. It won't hurt you to get something to eat with me."

"I am going to talk to you some other time."

"Whatever, there are plenty of women that would love for me to take them out to eat; you don't know a good thang when you see it."

"Bye, Tyree."

Men are a trip. Sounds like he has control issues. He acted like he was going to make me go out to eat with him. I have made up my mind I definitely would not be calling him. I checked my voice mail before I got in the shower.

Leave a message at the tone.

(Beep) "Momma, tell Chris I got a ride home." (Beep) "You know who this is, ya boy, call me." (Beep) "Special, this Tyree I guess if you're not going to let your fingers do the walking, I won't be calling to do the talking." (Beep) "Hey Sweetie this is Mercedes, call a sista, I got to tell you about what Koby and I did the other day."

Tyree was definitely crazy. I hoped he would lose my phone number real quick. I wondered when he had left that message. I hoped he would not let his fingers dial my number anymore, stupid punk. He was the kind of man women sometimes put up with just to have someone in their life. Since I had been there and done that with Chucky, I recognized the pattern right away and knew I had to run in the other direction. I refused to talk to him anymore. He was acting crazy and I will not put up with that type of behavior again. That is what I get for thinking I would use him to get over Busta. I know I have to pay attention to the red flags and the warning signs now. I refused to hang in there for two years and suddenly realize the man has gone psycho. I ignored the signs, downed played them, and in the long run accepted them while I was with Chucky. I will never do that again. I realize the earlier I pay attention to the signs; the better off I would be in the long run. Don't let meeting a man like Tyree keep in an unhealthy relationship. I almost started to convince myself I did not want to get to know anybody else after Busta. I wanted to avoid meeting men like Tyree and afraid to meet another man like Chucky.

> *"First you try to find a reason, try to understand what you've done so wrong so you can be sure not to do it anymore. After that you look for signs of a Jekyll and Hyde situation, the good and the bad in a person sifted into separate compartments by some weird accident. Then, gradually, you realize that there isn't a reason, and it isn't two people you're dealing with, just one. The same one every time."*

~ Helen Oyeyemi

I met Chucky after my relationship with Ike ended. He was from California, seemed nice and was very handsome. He was different from all the other guys I had met, and I liked the fact that I did not have to worry about anybody I knew, knowing him. I will never forget when his aggressive side started showing. The signs were there in the beginning. I just ignored them, made excuses for the behavior, and justified them.

One day Chucky and I were in the car when an argument started. Chucky was getting angry and I could see the veins in his neck popping out and it looked like they were throbbing. I sat still while my heart began beating faster and faster. He pounded on the steering wheel. I sat there afraid to speak and afraid he would start pounding on me. His mouth was moving but I could not understand him since I was focusing on his veins and his fists. He had the meanest and the most evil expression on his face. He was driving like a mad man while still controlling the car. I continued to sit still since I was afraid to say anything. He started asking me questions and I was not sure if I should answer. I did not want to speak in case I said something wrong that might have made him angrier. He started yelling, and acting crazier than usual. When we got home, he went straight to the bathroom. I stayed in the living room and tried to figure out what to do. I was nervous and scared. I did not know what to expect. I got the boys ready for bed while trying to be very quiet. I did not hear him come out of the bathroom and was surprised to see him sitting on the edge of the bed staring at me. I was not sure how long he had been there, he was too quiet, and his eyes did not even blink. He said something, but I did not hear him. He yelled, "Answer me", in a very mean tone. I told him I did not hear him. He got even more upset and said, "Yes you did!" I went to the living room and started pulling out the boy's fold out bed. At that time we lived in a one-bed room apartment. He told me to come back to the bedroom. As I walked in the room he raised his fists towards me like he was going to hit me, but he did not touch me. I screamed, then jumped, and stumbled across the floor, and started crying. I tried to move out of his way, but he kept blocking me. I thought about the children hearing what was going on in the room, and I was sure they were very afraid. I heard my boys crying before he closed the bedroom door. I was too frightened to move. He continued to wave his fists at me then began pounding on the wall. Every time he moved toward me I flinched and hoped he would not hit me. My heart was pounding while tears streamed down my face. He got angrier because I would not stop crying. Once I stopped he approached me and acted like he wanted to pound on me. This went on for what seemed like hours. My boys continued to cry and I was too afraid to fight back. I wanted to hold my boys and tell them everything would be okay. He looked so mean and evil I was afraid to look at him. My boys kept asking for me throughout this whole ordeal until they fell asleep. He told them to go to sleep and not answer the phone. I remember crying harder because I could not reach out to them and I could not help myself. I tried not to imagine what they were thinking. They probably thought he was hitting me. I hated him for what he was doing. I kept thinking I would kill him if I could because he was acting crazy and out of control. I wanted to find a way to end the terror. I kept wondering why he had not hit me. I did not know what he was going to do from one minute, to the next. He was torturing me. He went back into the bathroom and was in there for a very long time. I sat on the bed too scared to move or do anything. I could not hear the children anymore and I got up enough nerve to check on them. Thank goodness they had finally cried themselves to sleep. It was three o'clock in the morning. I got in the bed with my clothes on, cried myself to sleep and begged God to keep my boys and me safe. I did not know when Chucky came out of the bathroom. When we got up the next morning to get the children ready for school, he acted like nothing ever happened. He was actually in a good mood. I started blaming myself and wondered what I had done or said to make him flare up the way he did. I will never forget that night. I wished he had beat me and gotten it over with, instead of torturing me.

This was one of several moments when Chucky showed me his evil side. Sometimes he would get angry with me for days at a time and I would not understand why. I read cards and letters years later that described how bad he made me feel. I was shocked at what I had written.

At first some of the things he did I just took as being cool. I convinced myself that it was because he really liked me. I acted like it meant nothing because it was too early in the relationship to say anything, hoping things would change. He would be upset if I took too long at the store. He threw personal things back in my face and used them against me, to make me feel worse. Chucky and I had several mental abusive incidents. Those incidents messed with my head and made me feel awful. Sometime he talked to me and kept asking questions, while his gun was in plain view on top of the radio speaker. Of course I could not speak freely, I was too afraid. I just said what I thought he wanted to hear. I ignored things and down played them in the beginning. I made a vow to myself to never ignore certain types of behaviors again. When a man displays signs of mental control pay attention and don't ignore it. In the end, those same things can destroy you. I had to be strong and protect my sons.

I convinced myself too many times that it was no big deal and things were fine. Chucky did not understand that his actions were causing damage to my boys and me mentally. In his mind because he had never physically hit me everything was just fine and that no damage had been done. Mental abuse cannot be seen and gets down played because there are no physical scars, no black eyes and no blood. Losing my hair in clumps or my stomach aching were signs of stress, that went unnoticed. It was so stressful not knowing what I would do or say that would set him off.

I wound up hating men like him.

One of my voice messages was from Busta. I have no desire to call him back.

9

IT'S A BOY

"I have a son, who is my heart. A wonderful young man, daring and loving and strong and kind."

~Maya Angelou

Dr. Smith was amazing. We had a good session today. I talked about my boys for most of the hour. She wanted to focus on something that made me smile. I could have gone on for hours about the boys. I wanted to talk about something else. I was thrown off because I was prepared to unload about all the horrible things that had happened in my life. When Dr. Smith wanted to hear about my sons I was not prepared. She wanted to know about what I was feeling when I first found out I was pregnant with all of them, being that I was so young when I had them.

"Hello Dr. Smith. I have some good news. I have not called or seen Busta."

"Why, do you believe that is good news? Do you think that means you do not love him anymore? Do you think that means you are over him? It takes more than that Special."

"I hope it is a sign. I feel proud of myself. He has called me, but I did not return his call. I am really finished with him this time."

"I do not think it is a sign. Let's talk about something positive for a change, let's talk about your children. Tell me about your first child. I want to know what happened when you found out you were pregnant and what was going on at the time."

"My first son is Patrick II. I remember feeling very tired all the time but did not understand why. It never occurred to me that I was pregnant. I was fourteen-years-old. I was not shocked like I imagined I would be once I found out I was pregnant. I had been taking care of my friend's children for so long. I guess the big change would be that the baby would not be going home. My mother did not have too much to say and acted like it did not matter. I do not remember her saying anything at all. I do not know if she cared that her fourteen-year-old daughter was pregnant. I was four months along when I found out. It was upsetting realizing that I was not upset or shocked that I was having a baby at such a young age. There was no guidance in my life and no talk about the do's and don'ts with boys.

I just tried to figure things out on my own. I wanted to feel loved by somebody and wanted some attention.

"This was not an intentional or planned pregnancy."

"Oh no, not at all!"

"Go ahead, tell me more."

"Once it was confirmed I was pregnant I continued feeling sick all the time. I wondered if this was all in my young imagination or was the sick feeling for real. I was told I was having a boy. I felt tired, extremely sleepy all the time and had no desire to get up and go to school, eventually I stopped going. I was only in the ninth grade. At birth, Patrick weighed five pounds, ten ounces and was eighteen inches long. He looked like a little Hispanic baby. I had been in labor for twenty-four hours. I was scared and very confused. I did not know whom he looked like. While in the delivery room, I started wondering when was I going back to school? I missed almost all of school that year. Then, I started thinking about what his father would think of him. My mother was probably high. She looked sleepy and very stressed out. I could not imagine what she was thinking or what was on her mind. She was not talking to me. She was falling to sleep. The nurse came in the room to tell my mother a police hold had been placed on the baby and me so momma was not allowed to take us from the hospital without the caseworker's permission. The words did not seem to bother her. She just continued to stare into space, did not show any interest or emotion and never asked any questions. I did not understand what was going on, so I did not ask any questions either. I was a child that could not even take care of myself let alone a newborn baby."

"A police hold was placed on you and the baby? If I am correct, that meant the two of you could not leave the hospital until the caseworker said it was okay? Did you and the baby go into a foster home from the hospital?"

"No. I went to Children's House from the hospital. Children's house is where young children are placed who have suffered abuse and/or neglect. I was there for about ten days before Patrick II joined me. Then we went to a foster home together. I remember before leaving the hospital I went to the nursery to look at Patrick II one last time. I could not find him because he looked like all the other Hispanic babies. I kept looking for him but could not find him. I started to panic and I thought the caseworker had taken him away from me. I began to cry and started asking the nurse where he was. Momma never visited us again in the hospital. One of the nurses pointed to my baby, and he was right by the window where I was standing. I felt bad because I did not recognize him. I was so young and immature. I smiled and started crying at the same time. I could not do anything about leaving him; it was not my choice. I begged God to please let everything be all right. I was officially in foster care and there were no other options, especially no more running away. I had a baby now and both of us needed someone to take care of us."

"What do you mean by no more running?"

"After the caseworker picked up my youngest sister Precious, my oldest sister Dimples and I were across the street watching what was going on when she came to take us away. We knew we would have to run if we thought she was coming across the street."

"How did the caseworker get Precious?"

"They picked her up from school. Precious did not like being in foster care. She blew several placements and had been on runaway status the last year and half she was in the system. Precious aged out at eighteen and was automatically released."

"Tell me what happened when you had your second son."

"My second son is Donte'. When I found out I was pregnant I remember thinking, "Oh my GOD, this is not happening to me again, I cannot be pregnant!" I thought about what was going to happen to Patrick's relationship with me because he was very young and we were so close. I hoped things would not change between us. I wondered what my foster mother would say. Would she kick us out? Would I be separated from my son? What would happen to us? What about school? I kept telling myself I could not go to school with a big belly. I was in so much trouble and did not know what to do. My mind kept racing and I wondered if I should tell anybody. Who would I tell? I did not know what to do and I was so scared. I knew I had really messed up. I tried to stop crying while I calmed down so I could think about my options. I did not know what I would do with a second child. I felt like my life was really messed up. I was too afraid to tell my caseworker and foster mother that I was pregnant. I knew they would be angry. I could not look anybody in the face. I tried to convince myself to make myself have a miscarriage. I thought of jumping off the roof and eating a lot of hot and spicy foods thinking that would make me have a miscarriage. I felt so stupid, hopeless and helpless."

"How did things go after the caseworker and your foster mother found out?"

"Well, it was not as bad as I had imagined. After I got past the funny and the disappointed looks, once everybody knew I wasn't so stressed about it anymore. My caseworker hoped the baby would be able to stay with me. There was talk about my children and me being separated if we could not be placed together. That scared me and made me angry. I started blaming my mother for everything I was going through. I got over being afraid that things would change between Patrick and me. Contact with my mother was nothing. I became determined to do something with my life. I got frustrated thinking that my children would end up with nothing like me. I wanted to give my children more than my mother had given me. I thought about the holidays and not being able to celebrate Christmas like everyone else did. I cried for my two children and me. I hoped I could make it with two children. My foster mother did not say much, but she did look disappointed. She told me she would keep me and my children together if she could."

"After Donte' was born, did you and the children get to stay together?"

"Yes, we were, thank God. When Donte' was born his weight was six pounds, twelve ounces and he was seventeen inches long. He was wide-eyed and pale with a smile on his little face. His father was taking pictures of our new son. My baby was looking around like he was searching for someone in particular. He had a curious look on his face. I could not believe his eyes were opened. I do not remember hearing him cry. He just kept looking around. Wow, another boy. He was so cute, but he was supposed to be a girl. I felt very bad for thinking about jumping off the roof and the consequences I would have suffered. I thought about how scared I was when I found out I was pregnant, and all the negative comments that got back to me. I could not remember what my caseworker had to say. I was so glad my second baby was coming home with me. There was no more talk about me being separated from my children. I told myself we would be all right, and I would make sure of it. Every night I begged God to keep me and the boys together and to make sure we would be okay."

"Let' talk about your third child. It was another boy, right?"

"My third son is Christopher. I asked God, why he let this happen to me again. I prayed that I would never get pregnant again. I bargained with God not to let this happen. I told him that I could not get pregnant since that was my last year of high school. I was finally caught up on all my credits to graduate on time with my senior class. I was afraid to tell the baby's father and I felt like I did not want to keep the baby. I did not know what to do. I told myself I would not tell anybody and I would figure it all out. My second son was only four months old. I knew I had screwed up royally and felt certain I was going to be separated from my children this time. There was no way we would be able to stay together. I knew God had nothing to do with my situation but I kept asking Him why He let this happen to me AGAIN. I told my school counselor first. She was encouraging, very supportive and never made me feel bad or ashamed. She never made me feel like I could not make it. I could tell by her expression that she would not judge me. She provided me with a waiver from my physical education class so I could graduate. She had already helped me sign up for classes that were sent in the mail and classes I could take early in the morning before regular classes began. She considered all options so I could graduate on time with my class. She knew I really needed a break in life and felt that if I graduated that would be a very good start for our future. She knew I was determined to graduate and she helped me. I had gone to summer school the two previous years. I stayed after school and took early classes to make up the credits I needed to graduate since I had no credits from my freshman year. I finished those credits over the three previous years. I could not let being pregnant stop me. The baby would be born before I walked across the stage on my graduation day. I had to get over feeling embarrassed and ashamed again. I easily got over what people said. I knew I was a good person who would be somebody no matter what people thought. I was very determined but I was still angry with myself for getting pregnant again. My anger quickly turned into motivation and determination that made it easier to get up for school every day. I breezed through my school assignments. My boyfriend made it clear he wanted me to keep the baby. He made sure I got to school and helped with lunch money. We talked about how confused he felt when I told him I was pregnant. He was concerned that I would not want to keep the baby and he was afraid to tell me how he felt because I lived in foster care. We were stressed about what would happen if I were moved into another foster home and about all kinds of things we had no control over. I hoped I could handle three children. I had another boy. Christopher weighed five pounds, ten ounces and was twenty inches long. He came out sucking his tongue. I was very tired and emotional after he was born. I thought to myself, not another boy. He was supposed to be Crystal my baby girl, I was very happy just the same. I thanked God that my new baby was coming home with me. I was not sure how I was going to handle three children under four years old.

Somehow I felt confident I could handle it all with a little help when I needed it. I hoped I would be able to love all three of my boys equally. I was not sure how to share my time and affection with the three of them. I cried at the realization I was about to face. Deep down inside I knew by the grace of God everything would be all right for the four of us, but I was scared. My foster mother once again said we would not be separated. All I could think about was how I had to do something to make things better for us. We had to have a better life than my sisters and I had. While I was still in the hospital I made a vow that my children would never go without, would never be taken away from me and would never go through what I experienced as a child. While crying, deep inside I felt God would watch over us and everything would be all right."

"It sounds like after your third son was born you knew more responsibility rested on your shoulders and that you had to finish school."

"Yes, after Christopher was born, I became even more determined to finish school and stay focused."

"Tell me about your last son."

"My youngest son is Michael Jr. I remember thinking Okay, God; I realize that you were not the one having unprotected sex. I know that after all the bargaining I did with you; you knew what I was going to do anyway. I took responsibility that one of the consequences for having unprotected sex is pregnancy. All the bargaining and praying in the world could not prevent it. I put myself in the situation and I am responsible for the consequences. I cried for a long time after I found out I was pregnant with Michael. I no longer blamed God for getting pregnant. I left the clinic with my head down. Not again was all I was thinking. I could not imagine me with four children. I kept asking myself was I crazy or something? I had lost my mind. My boyfriend at the time had an attitude problem. I knew he could get mad at me and be mad for several days over petty things. I really did not want to imagine his response after finding out I was pregnant. This definitely was not planned. I was glad I did not have to deal with foster mothers and caseworkers any longer. My boyfriend just hunched his shoulders and had a "whatever" expression on his face. I did not know how either of us felt. I was mad and felt very stupid for letting this happen again. I was not married, had no career, with my fourth child on the way. I repeated that to myself over and over again. I was so ashamed of myself and kept asking myself how I could let this happened one more time. I did not know how I was going to raise four children and give them everything I did not have. I did not have a clue. My eyes were filled with tears on a regular basis because I was so frightened. Not again, was all I kept thinking. Michael weighed three pounds, four ounces and was sixteen inches long. He cried immediately when he was born with one of his fists balled up very tightly like he was angry. He came two months early, born on the fourth of July. He was pale and very small but strong and very independent. He never needed oxygen to help him breathe. My water had broken early and I went into pre-labor several times. I was on complete bed rest at the hospital for two weeks. He decided he was coming and nobody was going to stop him. He remained in the hospital for over a month and got stronger every day. It took him no time to gain weight. I knew he would be my nightmare child. After watching him in the hospital for over a month, I knew I had to do something to make sure my children would have a good life. I was young, but I was a good mother. There had to be something I could do to secure our stability. I prayed to God that something good would happen for us. I knew we were overdue for better days ahead. I was determined to not depend on a man for security. That semester I started school at the community college in Los Angeles CA. I felt college would be my way out. I believed that if I could finish school, get a degree, I would get a good job, I truly believed that.

"You become what you believe."

~Oprah Winfrey

10

THE DECISION

Women who have undergone post-abortion counseling report over 100 major reactions to abortion. Among the most frequently reported are: depression, loss of self-esteem, self-destructive behavior, sleep disorders, memory loss, sexual dysfunction, chronic problems with relationships, dramatic personality changes, anxiety attacks, guilt and remorse, difficulty grieving, increased tendency toward violence, chronic crying, difficulty concentrating, flashbacks, loss of interest in previously enjoyed activities and people, and difficulty bonding with later children.

Among the most worrisome of these reactions is the increase of self-destructive behavior among aborted women. In a survey of over 100 women who had suffered from post-abortion trauma, fully 80 percent expressed feelings of "self-hatred."

In the same study, 49 percent reported drug abuse and 39 percent began to use or increased their use of alcohol. Approximately 14 percent described themselves as having become "addicted" or "alcoholic" after their abortions. In addition, 60 percent reported suicidal ideation, with 28 percent actually attempting suicide, of which half attempted suicide two or more times.

After several sessions with my therapist Dr. Smith, we continued talking about my sons and my personal life.

"During one session she asked "Did you ever consider birth control or having an abortion?"

"I do not know why I never thought about having an abortion when I was younger. More than likely it was due to religious reasons. I was young and not educated about sex or my options and was not educated about birth control. I do not recall it ever crossing my mind or thinking of it as an option. Before I got pregnant with Donte', my doctor prescribed several different brands of birth control pills and they all made me sick. I do not remember if I was still taking the pills when I became pregnant with Donte'. I had an abortion a couple of years ago."

"So you have had an abortion before? Why did you have one then?"

"I felt it was something I needed to do for my children. A decision that I thought was going to destroy me. There was no way I could afford another mouth to feed. We were living with my grandfather at the time. I had part time jobs and I was scared out of my mind. The father could not do anything to help; he did not have a job and was living with somebody else. When I was sick, he suggested I see a doctor under someone else's name to avoid the bill. I was so frightened and could not imagine taking care of another child by myself. I was on a limited income, and living with my Grandfather."

"What was that experience like for you?"

"It was difficult because I often told myself several times there were certain things I would never do and an abortion was one of them. I was out of options and felt very desperate. When I went to the clinic it appeared to be a regular doctor's office, not the horror stories I had heard about. There were no boycotters outside handing out information that provided pictures of unborn children being sucked into a vacuum. There was no one outside yelling at me or calling me a murderer. I envisioned people taunting, yelling, and cursing at me. I had heard a lot of stories about going to an abortion clinic. When I entered the clinic, there were several other women waiting in chairs. Some of the women were older than me. Most of them appeared to be very young. There was a much older white woman, another black woman and several young white girls. The white girls appeared unaffected by being there. The older woman had a sad look on her face and looked very scared. I wondered why they were there. I kept thinking and wanted to know if they were there to get an abortion or just a pregnancy test. I felt like they were staring at me, like they automatically knew why I was there. I was with my aunt. She was as supportive as a Christian could be. She was friendly with everybody in the clinic. I appreciated the fact that she never questioned my decision while we were there. She just listened to my many reasons for needing the abortion. I did not have a full time job, no medical insurance and I was very tired of being sick all the time. My children were concerned and kept asking what was wrong. I started spitting all day long; in the trash, in cups, and everywhere I could as an attempt to get the nasty taste out of my mouth. Nothing helped. Everything had an awful odor to it. I was constantly throwing up. I felt bad because I could not go to work to support my children. I was afraid that I would lose everything. I was afraid that I could not handle another child. In the long run it would cost too much to have another baby. I could not depend on my boyfriend to support us. My mind was racing a hundred miles a minute. I wanted to get up and just run out of the clinic. I kept thinking this baby was a girl, I even told my grandfather I thought it was a girl. Granddaddy was a man of few words. He did not ask any questions, he did not comment on my situation or offer any advice. My aunt, the rest of the ladies and I were waiting to be called to the next waiting area. The white lady that appeared to be scared and nervous was already in the next room as I entered. The room was small with a table full of brochures about babies, expecting mothers, decorating, and gardening. I noticed there were some pamphlets, on the table. When I picked up one of the pamphlets I thought I heard the lady say something. We just looked at each other in silence for a long time. She suddenly started talking, and I smiled trying to appear okay with the situation. She said she did not know if she was doing the right thing. She had gotten pregnant while she was separated from her husband. They had gotten back together but she was not sure if the baby was his or her lover's. I just listened because I was afraid of saying the wrong thing. The nurse called her to leave the room first. I sat there wondering what I would do if I was in her situation. It was interesting to hear of other people's reasons for visiting the clinic. I could not imagine being in her situation. Minutes later, I was called to another room. I was asked if I wanted to be put to sleep or just given some medication so I would not feel the procedure. I wanted to stay awake because the fear of dying on the table crossed my mind. I was convinced dying would be my punishment for having an abortion. I felt guilty and started thinking about dying if they put me to sleep. While lying on the table the nurse did the ultrasound to determine how far along I was. I thought about getting up and running. I thought I was at least ten weeks along. I heard her say, "You are six weeks." I told myself I had a little more time to think about it. Tears started welling up in my eyes. Since I was there and the process had begun. I started counting all the reasons for going through the process. I was really tired of throwing up and everything had a spoiled and rotten odor. I slept a lot to avoid feeling sick and spitting all the time. I could not take care of the boy's appropriately. I kept thinking about the reasons, over and over again. I had just graduated from college a couple of months prior to getting pregnant but still did not have a full-time job. Then I thought, "How did I get pregnant in the first place?" We were using protection. There was no need to bargain with God, I used protection. I remembered asking my boyfriend if the condom ever broke. While lying on the table I was feeling guilty, confused and ashamed. I remembered him saying "No", but a couple of times we did have sex without protection. I could not believe what I was hearing. "What? When? What are you talking about?" He told me on a couple occasions, he messed with me while I was asleep. He thought I knew because I would lay there like it was okay and didn't try to stop him. I got very upset, and my head started throbbing. I asked him what happened and he talked about having intercourse with me while I was asleep. I got extremely upset. My head started hurting more. I said I would have remembered if he had sex with me, I would have felt it. I started crying, felt very ashamed and consumed with guilt. I told him he was raping me in my sleep and I had no clue what he was talking about. He got upset and said he realized that I really could have been asleep during the whole experience because he was not sure if I responded or not. I became more upset and at that point I ended the conversation. Nothing was going to change my current situation.

I lay very still and stiff on the cold table. I could not move. Tears began rolling down both sides of my face. The vacuum sound of the machine was very loud. The doctor's hands were very cold. He explained every step of the process. I did not feel a thing and remained very silent. I lay there thinking it was too late; the procedure was done. I cried hysterically. When I was taken to another room I could hear my aunt consoling other girls. I could not stop crying. I heard somebody say, "If you don't cry, you're not human." "I see girls come in here every other month, the same girls, and they don't cry." "You'll be fine, just let it out." I lay there for at least thirty minutes, crying uncontrollably and non-stop. Then, I thought about the possibility of the baby being a girl. I felt like it was a girl and the thought made me cry even harder. Since I had never been that sick during my past pregnancies somehow I knew it was a girl. I became angrier with myself at the thought. The reasons why I was there came back to me. I questioned my faith in God. If it had been stronger I would have found a way to have and raise this baby. I got angrier and cried more. My aunt came to my side and said, "Ask Him to forgive you." I thought she had read my mind. I looked into her eyes and she said nothing else, she just patted my head and rubbed my back. I still felt sick to my stomach on the way home. I told myself all the symptoms from being pregnant were going to be over very soon now that the baby was gone. I held my stomach while constantly crying. My aunt did not utter a word during the ride home. I got home and the boys just stared at me. They did not know what I had done. They looked sad, and they were concerned for me. My baby asked if I was still sick. I felt guilty and ashamed while they stared at me. That night crazy thoughts kept coming to mind. The symptoms were still there and I knew my punishment would be to spit for the rest of my life, as if I was still pregnant. I stopped thinking about everything and cried myself to sleep balled up with my knees to my chest. My stomach felt empty and every time I woke up I still had to spit. My quick fix abortion was making me crazy. My mind was racing with all kind of thoughts. I tried not to think about it, but I could not stop, I cried more and kept seeing a little girl's face. I begged God for forgiveness. I could not reverse or undo anything. I desperately needed God to forgive me because I was sorry, truly sorry. I allowed myself to feel the anger, shame, guilt, embarrassment, and helplessness. When I woke up the next morning the spitting had stopped. My head felt heavy but I was light headed at the same time. I did not know what to do with myself. I put what energy I had into taking care of my boys."

"There will be rough nights but joy really does come in the morning."

~ **Tyler Perry**

"You are opening up a lot. It is good that you are crying, go on."

"I thought I would never get over that abortion Dr. Smith, never. Several months later I felt like the whole ordeal was still haunting me. When thoughts of the abortion entered my mind, I had to cut them off before I started crying. For days, I imagined what she would have looked like. I gave her a name. I asked her to forgive me. It took a month but I finally stopped crying when I thought about her."

"Sounds like you processed that traumatic experience very well, on your own. An abortion is not easy and some people never get over it. I will see you next week. Feel free to call me sooner if you need to."

"Thank you, I will, Dr. Smith."

"You have been blessed with wonderful young men. You did what you felt you had to do at that time. Continue to let go."

"I will thanks again."

11

OVERCOMING SEXUAL ABUSE

It is normal for victims to freeze and be unable to physically fend off their abuser.

Effects of Sexual Assault: Post traumatic Stress, Self Harm, Flashbacks, Depression, Substance Use,

For the survivors, but for those around them. During a 'flashback', the survivor re-experiences the sexual abuse as if it were occurring at that moment. It is usually accompanied by visual images, or flashes of images, of the abuse. This is one of the ways of remembering the abuse.

Flashbacks are often triggered by an event, action, or even a smell that is reminiscent of the sexual abuse or the abuser.

Feelings of extremely low self-esteem or self-hatred are common in survivors. Extreme depression is something with which survivors also battle.

A s soon as I got home the phone rang. It was my girl Mercedes.

"Hey Mercedes, I just got home, what's up?"

"I called to see how you have been doing in therapy? You have been going for a while now and I want to know if it is helping, because of my internship in Psych."

"I cannot tell yet but I do know it has made me remember a lot of things I do not like to think about."

"What are you telling her? I know you go on and on about Busta."

"I mentioned Busta, but we did not go into details about him today. I have not talked to him either. We talked about the children today. I wanted to talk about being sexually abused to get it over with and see what she has to say. She's always analyzing me."

"How many people have you told you were sexually abused? This is news to me. Why didn't you tell me?"

"Not too many people know. I will just explain it to you. It is not something that I like to think or talk about. I get angry and emotional when I think about it."

"Who sexually abused you? I know your father died when you were a baby, didn't he?"

"It was one of my mother's boyfriends. I remember he was old with gray hair and had a fat stomach. The more he came around, the funnier he looked. After he had been seeing my mother for a few months, she started leaving us alone with him. I had put anything and everything about him out of my mind until one day I woke up with a really bad headache. I was standing in the kitchen and Chucky had followed me murmuring something about if I did not want to have sex I could have just said something. He told me about the things he did to me while I was asleep. I was not responding to him and did not do anything to stop him. He said that was not the first time I had done him like that."

"What did you say to him?"

"I just looked at him like he was crazy. Then he said, he knew I felt what he was doing to me, and I could have said that I did not want to have sex. I turned to look at him and he walked away. I stood looking out the kitchen window thinking to myself that if he had done those things to me I would have felt it. I was getting angry and kept repeating to myself thinking he was kidding. Then, I became very frustrated trying to remember if he had touched me. I realized how upset he was about it. I kept telling myself I would have known because I would have felt it. I walked into the living room and sat down on the sofa. I told myself again that if Chucky had done those things to me I would have felt it. Somehow I knew he was telling me the truth. My head started hurting. I felt confused and I started breathing faster. I repeated it again "If he had done those things to me I would have felt it." I started having memories of being in my mother's boyfriend's car. I looked back at the car and told myself he was lying, because I would have felt it if he had done those things to me. I heard him say, "Do you remember what I did to you?" I could see myself sitting very still in a car. The whole experience was weird and crazy. He gave me a blow-by-blow account of the things he say he had done to me. When some of the memories came back I put my head down in shame. I could not remember what he was talking about, because if he had done those things to me I would have felt it. I saw myself jumping out of the car."

"You did not remember until after Little Michael was born?"

"It was scary and crazy at the same time. It was like I went back in time or something. I was either twenty-one or twenty-two when I remembered. It was very confusing. I remember being on the living room floor crying and shaking. I could see me waking up with my shorts pulled down around my thighs and my mother asking me why my pants were down when I woke up. I could not even answer her. I just looked at her like she was crazy. I remember being in a deep sleep. It was like I could see myself looking at her. She looked away from me. Nothing was ever said about my clothes being down again."

"I am sorry that happened to you Sweetie. What happened after that and where was Chucky?"

"I do not know where Chucky went, he probably got angry and left. It is all very vague but I kinda started remembering my mother asking her boyfriend to give me a ride down the street. While I was in the car with him, he told me what he had done to me the weekend before. My mother left him to babysit my little sister and me. I started remembering him pulling my clothes down. It was like I was having flashbacks. It was scary and I could not breathe. I remember falling asleep and when I woke up my pants were down. My head was hurting real bad by the time I remembered. I did not want to believe it was true. My head started hurting worse and my stomach began to hurt. I cried while the memories came flooding back. I just knew for sure none of it could be true. I asked myself several times if it was true. I could not remember how old I was, or any more details."

"Oh my God, What did you do after that? Are you okay?"

"I did not do anything. I felt hurt and very ashamed. I was angry, confused, frustrated, and felt very unprotected. All the energy I had drained out of my body. I got off the sofa and tried not to think about it but my thoughts kept jumping all over the place."

"Why are you crying?"

"That is something you can never get over; I do not care how long ago it happened. It's like your body is in the moment and the feelings are present. I wanted to talk to Dr. Smith because I wanted to see what she would have to say about it."

"Why didn't you tell me? You sound like you are upset like it just happened."

"After being sexually assaulted on any level, you do not ever get over it. The talk shows host, Oprah is over forty years old and she still gets upset and teary eyed about her ordeal. I get emotional and other people I know do as well when they think about what happened to them."

"You will be alright. I cannot believe you did not tell me."

"I do not know why I did not tell you Mercedes, I try not to think about it."

"Keep me posted about your therapy. I start seeing patients in about a week. I love my internship and think I found my passion. I will have my bachelor's degree by the end of the year. When you talk to Dr. Smith about the abuse, please tell me what she had to say. You know we can talk about anything, anytime."

"I will. I am so glad you are graduating soon, that is some good news, and I cannot wait. I know I need to go back to school. How is your mother?"

"She is fine, over there being all prissy. You know how she is."

"Yeah, prissy fits her. I will talk to you later I need to lie down. Oh how are things with Koby?"

"I saw him, and after seven years of drama I should be tired by now. I have too much going on to keep this up with him. He is not going to change. I am busy with school right now anyway. I have enough to keep me occupied with no time to deal with him. I think I have truly had enough. We both tell ourselves that if one or the other can stay in that kind of relationship then it is okay to keep doing what we are doing. Bye Sweetie, I will call you this weekend."

Mercedes is so right. I feed off her going back to Koby, so I keep going back to Busta like it is okay. I keep telling myself I will not go back after what he did the last time and he can just forget about me. He never appreciated me as a good woman and just uses other woman now. I was always doing for him before I did for myself. That was so stupid. He knew all along while he was letting me do things for him he was a dog and was not doing right by me. I wish I had a father to teach me about men and give me that male perspective. I hope my boys never treat woman like I have been treated.

I do not know why I never told Mercedes about the sexual abuse. I try not to think about it because I get so upset and feel so embarrassed. Those thoughts make my skin crawl, the hairs on my back and arms stick up, and I want to cry. I feel like curling up in a ball and hiding from the world. I remember lying on the bed on my stomach that night. I could feel him pulling at my pants but I was afraid to say or do anything. He was not saying anything either and I tried to pretend I was asleep. That did not stop him from pulling at my pants. I tried pushing myself deeper into the bed somehow thinking that would make it harder for him to unbutton my pants. When he got my pants undone,

I was scared and was screaming "no" to myself. He continued touching me while trying to open my legs. I tried to sink lower into the bed hoping he would stop. I needed my mother to come through the door. I have no idea what my sisters were doing or where they were.

I cannot remember if they were in the same bed or not. We slept in our daily clothes when it was bedtime and fell asleep wherever we were in the house. The buttons on my pants were undone and I did not know what to do. I just froze. I'm screaming no, but he can't hear me. He was still trying to open my legs when he started caressing me. My legs were side by side and I remained still and as stiff as I could while hoping he would stop. He scooted one of my legs to the side and the tears started falling down the sides of my face. It was dark; I felt smothered and held my breath for a very long time. I wanted him to think I was asleep, so I was afraid to move. He put his finger where he should not have and I silently cried harder than I ever had in my life. When I woke up the next morning, my mother asked why my pants were undone. I was half asleep and told her I did not know. She looked at me with a blank stare and turned away. I was able to breathe again and the night before was all a blur.

Memories from when I was twelve or thirteen years old and was sexually abuse came flooding back. At the time it was going on, I had no idea it was sexual abuse. As an adult I have a hard time understanding why a grown man would sleep with a little girl. I was about twenty-six years old and working in the convenience store of a gas station when I remembered. The memories came back when the man that abused me walked into the store. I was standing at the cash register when he told me to put $20.00 on pump number five. I froze when I recognized him. I held my breath and could not move. I was shaking and panic took over all at once. I ran to the back office and began crying. I did not understand why I was crying and felt so nervous. I had to sit down. I was around twelve or thirteen and he was twenty-one when we were involved. I suddenly realized that being with an older man would affect me for the rest of my life. I was young and naïve. I had no idea it was wrong because no one ever told me it was not right. He was not just some older guy from the projects. He was someone I thought I liked, back in the day. It seemed very cool and okay to hang out with a man almost twice my age. I was caught up with us liking each other. Small groups of us hung out in the back of the projects. In my mind we were just hanging out together. Everything was fun and seemed very cool. This made me feel like I was in with older people. Suddenly I remembered having sex with him. I was nervous and scared but I never made him stop because I felt comfortable and very special around him. He would never do anything to hurt me. He always offered to buy me things, but I do not remember if he ever did. He told me how mature I was and how he enjoyed my well-developed body. I had never heard anything bad about him and everybody we hung out with liked him. I thought it was so cool back in the day to be with him. My head started throbbing at the thought of a grown man having sex with a minor. My skin felt like ants were crawling all over me, suddenly I was overwhelmed with emotion at the thought of the twelve year-old little girl I was having insecure feelings about was me. I suddenly felt sick and in my head I was screaming, "he raped me, he's a child molester, he used me". I could not understand what I was thinking at twelve to have sex with a grown man. At twenty-six the reality of it all was very disgusting. I tried to make sense of a grown man hanging out with a minor but I could not. I felt so ashamed not only for myself, but for him as well. I felt used and violated and wondered how he could do that to a child. I became very angry. Confusion took over while my mind was racing all over the place about the disgusting thought. My body could not take it any longer and I wanted to throw up. I had to regain my composure and needed to get back to work. I wanted to grab a glass bottle of juice and throw it in his face, but I could not go out there and look at him. I checked the security screen to make sure he was gone. For days, I felt so used and abused. I was totally ashamed of myself.

Sexual abuse happens on different levels and in many different ways. Young girls must realize that even if it seems cool at the time it definitely is not. As a child hanging out with an older man, imagine the man being your father, uncle, or brother being with a little girl. The thought should be disgusting. Older men have no business hanging out with younger girls; they need to imagine that young girl being their niece or daughter. Men that consider using young girls for sex are child molesters no matter how they try to justify it. Young girls that believe older men want them as a companion need to understand that it is just about the sex or what they can get them to do. It does not matter how they convince you it is okay or how much money they spend on you. Older men are willing to tell younger girls what they want to hear and are manipulating them to get what they want physically. They can hone in on a young girl's low self-esteem and insecurities and play into that. If your parents are allowing you to hang out at night with a group of guys and other girls, the guys know your parents are not paying attention, and think they can do what they want with you. I was one of those younger girls that fell for the lies because I just wanted to be liked by somebody, anybody. I believed that he would buy me things that I did not have or my mother could not afford. Unfortunately, I did not have any parental supervision and was free to roam and hang out with whomever I pleased. My mother should have known the people I was with and where I was every minute of every day and night. I always know where my children are, whom they are with, and what they are doing, even as they get older.

At twelve I was an immature little girl in a woman's "looking" body. My mother was not providing for me. I was offered and promised things. I hung around hoping he would fulfill all he had promised. I was too young and naïve to realize I was being used and lied to. I was not getting any attention at home and this man told me how cute and fine I was. In my mind I knew what I was doing and thought I could handle it. I started craving the attention and liked it more and more. I wanted to hang around just hoping and waiting for the promises to be fulfilled. I could not imagine why he would lie to me. Not once did I consider our age difference. I actually thought it was cute and thought I was doing something cool. Oh, I thought I had something that my friends did not have. I believed that I was doing something that made me cool and a much better person. That was the mind of a twelve year old. I thought he wanted to be with me because he liked me. I was physically more developed than the rest of the girls my age. I started hating my body because it usually attracted trouble that I was not mature enough for. Yes, I liked and craved the attention but I was not mature enough to understand what was happening. The guys I attracted were interested in my body and not me as a person. They looked past me being a child.

> *"Young girls are like helpless children in the hands of amorous men, whatever is said to them is true and whatever manipulation on*

their bodies seems like love to them, sooner or later, they come back to their senses, but the scars are not dead inasmuch as her spoiler lives."

~Michael Bassey Johnson

12

FINDING PEACE WITH MY FATHER'S DEATH

The events that took place when I was twelve made me wish my father had been around to protect me. Why did Mercedes have to mention my father's death? I would like to think I would not have been sexually abused if he had been alive. I am sure my life would have been much better all-around in my opinion. With my dad in my life I probably would have had a better understanding about men. I would hope I would have been protected. I use to grab a pillow, bump my head against the couch or bed, and cry for him when things went wrong. I can say that God is good though because I was able to meet my daddy's mother before she died. I will always believe that God played a role in setting that up. I learned that you never know what or where your journey could lead you. If I had not gone to

California with my son's father, I probably would have never met her.

I remember so clearly how she answered the phone with a soft voice the first time I called her. She asked, "Who is calling?" I hesitated before answering because I was afraid of her response. When I told her who I was, she paused. Her only reply was, "I have been looking for you." She said it with a lot of compassion and enthusiasm. There was a little flutter in the pit of my stomach while tears filled my eyes. I was very relieved knowing she knew who I was and was interested in seeing me as much as I needed to meet her. She asked questions about my mother. She told me that my father was my aunt's boyfriend before I was born. Nobody could explain how my mother got pregnant by my aunt's boyfriend, only grandma knew. We talked for hours like we had been in each other's lives forever. We talked about how I found her, which was through a friend I met in college. She had a class with my cousin but I did not know she was my cousin. My friend told me there was a woman in her class with the same last name. I knew we had to be related because the last name is very uncommon and unique. We exchanged information and a lot of what my mother shared with me was consistent with what she said. As we continued our conversation, I felt like I had found what I had been searching for but was left with an empty feeling as well. The more we talked the more it felt like I had known her forever. As I continued to talk to my grandmother, I learned more about my father. She called other family members and we had several three-way conversations for the rest of the evening. Without hesitation my cousin Mario welcomed me into the family. We instantly clicked and started making plans to see each other soon. Mario and my grandmother made me feel wanted. I felt like I was finally a part of something real from my father. It felt like I was watching a movie. After all, nothing like this had ever happened to me before. I shed many tears with every family member I spoke with. It was hard to believe this was happening to me. For as long as I could remember I wished my father was still alive. The joy of actually having one of my prayers answered was overwhelming.

When we finally met in person we both started crying. We spent several holidays together and kept in touch. She added something very special to my life. She attended my graduation ceremony when I got my bachelor's degree and spent mother's day with me that year. It is amazing how things work out. I truly believe that God had something to do with it all. Some things could be considered coincidental and some things are from God. Grandma died a few months after I graduated from college.

I lay there and thanked the Lord for all the good that has happened in my life. It was a blessing from Him to have such wonderful children and the God given strength to work two jobs, while attending my son's ball games, taking them on errands and the ability to keep the house clean. I asked that He please remove anything and anyone negative from my life. I asked for forgiveness for any wrongdoing whether intentional or not. I wanted God to continue to bless my entire family and keep us safe. I begged for forgiveness for not paying attention when it came to Busta. I ignored all the signs and refused to let go of such a hurtful relationship. I promised to let him go for good and to never get involved with him again no matter what.

The traffic was terrible that day which frustrated me because I knew I was going to be late for work. That frustration brought up other frustrations about this and that. Feelings that had been buried had surfaced and I was trying to prevent being emotional. Then, when I arrived at work, I could not log on my computer system to work on my reports. I decided to check my e-mail while waiting for the computer technician.

You've got mail:

MERCEDES.COM: "What's up girl? I thought you might like this. I will call you later tonight." See Attachment:

"Woman to Woman"

Another woman will always be prettier. She will always be smarter. Her house might be bigger than yours and her car a newer model. Her children will do better in school. And her husband will fix more things around the house. So, let it go, and love yourself and your circumstances. The prettiest woman in the world can have turmoil in her heart. The most highly favored woman on your job may be unable to have children. The richest woman you know, who has the most expensive car, the biggest house, and all the latest fashion designer clothes, just might be lonely. The world may lead a woman to believe if she doesn't have love, she has nothing. So, love yourself for the person you are. Look in the mirror every morning, smile and say, "I am too blessed to be stressed and too anointed to be disappointed."

"Winners make things happen. Losers let things happen. To the world you might be one person, but to one person you just might be the world."

"Be Blessed ladies and pass this on to encourage other women."

– Unknown Author

Hmmmm! That is something to think about. If I read uplifting empowering thoughts like that everyday, I would not have time for drama in my life. I would feel stronger and more confident. The e-mail had strong valid points. I decided to print it and put it on my desk.

SPECIAL.COM: Thanks Mercedes, just what I needed to start my workday. I will talk to you soon. I think you will like this one." See attachment:

"A Good Woman"

A good woman is proud of herself, respects herself and others. She is aware of who she is. She neither seeks confirmation from the person she is with, nor does she expect them to read her mind. She is quite capable of articulating her needs. A good woman is hopeful. She is strong enough to make all her dreams come true. She knows love therefore she gives love. She recognizes that her love has great value and must be reciprocated. If her love is taken for granted, it soon disappears. A good woman has a dash of inspiration and a pinch of endurance. She knows she will at times have to inspire others to reach the potential God gave them. A good woman knows her past, understands her present, and moves toward her future. A good woman knows that with God the world is her playground, but without God she will be played with. A good woman does not live in fear of the future because of her past. Instead, she understands that her life experiences are merely lessons, meant to bring her closer to selfknowledge and unconditional self-love. I just sent this to "A Good Woman". Why don't you?"

~Unknown Arthur

I keep powerful e-mails like this around me all the time. I try to stay focused on ways to empower myself and stay focused. Reading e-mails like this one has given me strength when I was feeling down.

13

DOMESTIC VIOLENCE

Abuse can have a serious impact on the way a person thinks and interacts with the world around them. The chronic exposure to domestic violence—and the stress fear resulting from this exposure—can cause not only immediate physical injury, but also mental shifts that occur as the mind attempts to process trauma or protect the body. Domestic violence affects one's thoughts, feelings and behaviors and can significantly impact one's mental stability. Increased anxiety, post-traumatic stress disorder and depression symptoms are commonly observed among survivors of domestic violence.

I only worked one job today and scheduled a therapy appointment.

"Hello, this is Dr. Smith, whose calling?"

"Hello, this is Special, I forgot to unblock the number, sorry. Do you have a minute to talk?"

"Can you come to the office right now?"

"Yes, I will be there in about thirty minutes."

As I drove to Dr Smith's office, I tried to decide what I wanted to talk about. I noticed a lady running down the middle of the street. I could not see what or whom she was running from. All of a sudden I saw a man catch up to her and started pounding on her back right there in the middle of the street. I was glad to see the police coming. Watching that incident made me glad I was no longer in an abusive relationship.

When I arrived at Dr. Smith's office, I could not wait to tell her what I had just witnessed.

"Hi Dr. Smith, I just saw a man chasing a lady and beating on her in front of everybody in the middle of the street."

"Why are you so upset about it? Why are you breathing so hard?"

"I remember when I was in an abusive relationship. I think I am going through the emotions because I know how it feels."

"Let's talk about what happened to you."

"I really do not know where to begin. (pause) There was one incident when one of my son's father, Ike, beat me when he came home early in the morning after being out all night. He was supposed had been with his cousins. He got irritated because I did not respond the way he wanted me to when he tried to talk to me. He acted like I was not supposed to be mad because he was out all night. While I was getting ready for work he tried to kiss me. I asked him to get out of my face, and leave me alone. He kept trying to kiss me anyway. I got angry, and tried to walk away which annoyed him. He kept asking me why was I acting different and why I was trying to ignore him. I knew I could not tell the truth and say that I knew he was lying. If I had, it would have been hell to pay. He shoved me with all his might anyway from him. I wanted to be left alone because I knew he had lied to me. I could feel it. I got nervous and I tried to get out of his way. He got furious and blocked me from moving around in the bedroom. I kept telling him to let me get ready for work and to leave me alone every time he tried to hug or kiss me. He hit me in my back with his fist, and at that point, I was too afraid to say anything else. When I tried to leave he shoved me back into the room. I tried to calm him down but nothing worked. I asked him where he had been all night hoping he would back off. He said, "Just with my cousins." I asked why he did not call to let me know he was not ready to come home. He told me he had lost track of time. I called him a few times but he never answered. I figured he got upset because he felt guilty. Ike knew he was out of line. I knew he was guilty of something, and tried to reverse the situation on me. Instead of me being angry, he was the one who became furious. I tried to figure out what I had said or done wrong."

"That is probably true; he may have been guilty of something."

"He asked me why I was tripping. I told him I knew he was not with his cousins. He got angrier and told me to shut up. He grabbed the plastic stick that was a piece of the children's tent and hit me on my legs. Welts appeared immediately. I started crying and begged him to leave me alone."

"Did he leave you alone or get angrier?"

"He got angrier and slapped my face because I stared at him and would not speak. He slapped me so hard I saw stars. He apologized while I cried uncontrollably. I was so furious and defenseless. He told me, I was not going to work so we could work it out. He wanted to have sex and I was too afraid to turn him down so I didn't say no. During sex I felt like I was being used and raped. I cried the whole time and was miserable because of all the pain I was in from being hit. I just let him do whatever he wanted to do to me. I hated him and wanted to kill him. Several hours later, I waited for him to turn his back to me so I could leave and run to my grandmother's house. I was afraid to look back the whole time I was running. My heart was pounding very fast at the thought of what he had done the last time he beat me."

"My goodness Special, that was not the first time he punched and slapped you? Calm down, everything is okay, you are safe here."

"No, the last time he thought some guys in the park was flirting with me while I ran a lap around the tennis courts. When we got back home from the park he wanted to know what the guys were saying to me while I was running. I told him I had no idea because

I was not paying them any attention. He got angry and told me I liked the attention they were giving me. He went on and on about it, got in my face and started yelling. I tried to ignore him and that is when the shoving started. I told him to move, but he would not. He was full of rage and pushed me a second time. He called me stupid while I told him to leave me alone but he wouldn't. I was scared and very nervous since we were home alone. My heart beat faster and faster. He would not stop so when I turned to walk away, he grabbed my arm. I tried pulling away but couldn't, after all I am only five feet tall and weigh about 128 pounds. I asked him to leave me alone again and told him I did not want to fight. I knew I was no match for him and that frightened me more. I became more alarmed while thinking about the previous time we fought. That time he hit me harder than he had before. I knew I did not want to leave home with black eyes and scars from trying to fight back. I kept telling him to leave me alone. That only made him more hostile and he pushed me harder. I tried pushing him back then I hit him in the jaw and heard a snap. I started running away while he chased me down the apartment stairs. He caught up to me and the next thing I knew, I was getting up off the ground. I figured he had knocked me out. Once I shook off the lightheaded feeling, I ran back up the stairs and locked myself in the bedroom. He pounded on the door so hard I thought he was going to break it down. He demanded that I open it. I was too afraid not to let him in. He said he was sorry, begged for forgiveness and swore it would not happen again. I cried the whole time he was talking. I tried to ignore him while he continued to talk to me as though nothing serious had happened. I just sat there in silence and cried harder. I did not respond to anything he said. I could not believe he had the nerve to ask me to make a hamburger for him. I silently walked into the kitchen and started cooking."

"Why did you fix the hamburger?"

"I was afraid he would get mad again if I did not do what he asked. I thought about poisoning him. I wanted to hate him for filling me with so much anger and for making me feel helpless and scared. I decided to never fight back because the bruises and other marks on my body were not worth it. I did not want my children to see any evidence of being beaten. I thought about the fact every time we fought, he became more violent and began hitting me harder every time. After a while he came in the kitchen and said something that made me laugh. I was not angry anymore."

"Was that the last time he beat you, when you ran to your grandmother's house?"

"Yes it was. I decided I was not going to take it any longer. I ended the relationship and never looked back. I am glad I have not been in a situation like that since then."

"Is that what you came to talk about?"

"No, seeing that lady run down the street reminded me of my own experiences."

"How have you been? Are things okay?"

"Yes, everything is fine."

"Did you want to talk about Busta today?"

"No, that's okay. Just a second, my phone keeps
vibrating."

14

"Momma love me, pop left me."

~Jay Z

After checking my phone I wondered why Patrick could not wait for our evening talk to get in touch with me. I hoped it was not too serious.

"Hello."

"Momma this me I really need to talk to you, I need to talk right now."

"Hold on Pat, I am with Dr. Smith right now."

"Sorry Dr. Smith, Patrick is on the line, I have to leave. I can hear it in his voice, something is wrong."

"All right Special, make another appointment before you leave."

"I will thanks."

I made an appointment and sat in the car so Patrick could tell me what was so urgent.

"Go ahead Patrick. What is going on?"

"Man, life just ain't right momma. If life was right, then things would be plain and simple. I've tried to do the right thing but it doesn't matter. People don't get a choice at some things. It's not fair."

"What are you talking about Patrick?"

"My friends and I were at a club the other night minding our own business. These guys were at the club trippin'. When we got ready to leave one of them said my friend bumped into him. Momma they really tried to fight us. I'm getting tired of guys trippin'. I was ready to fight even though they are bigger than us. They blocked our car so we couldn't leave then tried to pull the car doors open, like they were really trying to get at us. We thought they were going to break the windows."

"Patrick, what did you do when they tried to get in?"

"Nothin', we kept trying to leave momma, there were too many of them, we not stupid! One of my homies tried to shoot at them but the gun didn't go off. The girl that was blocking our car finally moved and we drove off. Some girl must have given them my number because they started calling me and making threats on my phone. I've been trying to chill out, but now I'm fed up. See, if I would have took off on one of those punks from day one or if I had shot at them they would have chilled out by now. I'm down here thinking about the consequences and worrying about not doing anything that I know will hurt you. But being the nice guy doesn't work all the time. I have been chillin' all week. They done brought that shit; I mean stuff to my school momma."

"You be careful Patrick."

"I've been real careful. Momma I'm getting frustrated. This is some bull. It wasn't even me who pushed that guy. Now they are calling and threatening me. They probably made that pushing stuff up, just to make some trouble. It's probably about some broad. In a minute momma I'm going to do something and somebody might end up dead."

"I hope it does not come to that. I know you know what to do. I am going to trust that you will do the right thing."

"I've been doing the right thing. The right thing doesn't work all the time. If doing the right thing matters, your life would have been a lot easier. I've watched you do the right things all your life and you still have a hard time. Life isn't fair like adults try to make it seem. For instance, some people who go to college and earn degrees sometimes end up jobless. What's up with that? If it was that plain and simple to just go to school, get a degree, you should be able to get a good job because you did what you were supposed to do right! Life doesn't work like that momma. Look how that girl made Busta lose his job as a juvenile assistant by tellin' lies about him. Busta was good with those kids at Children's House. In a flash his career was taken from him because of some stupid broad. If life was fair, that wouldn't have happened to him. I can see if he wasn't good with those kids, but he was. Life ain't right momma."

"You know Patrick I can understand that, but do not become a bitter person who makes bad choices because eventually the decisions we make catch up with us."

"Okay then, why did God let Busta come into your life knowing he wasn't going to be right for you? You weren't looking for Busta when he came to you. He pursued you and look what happened. He knew his situation before stepping to you. He did things that were not right and that had nothing to do with you, but God knew he was going to hurt you, right? You weren't out at a club when you met Busta. I've watched how you have helped other people all your life, done right by them, done the right things, and life still hasn't treated you right. Now what?"

"Look Patrick, I do not know what kind of decisions you are thinking about making. I really cannot say much because I am not there, but I hope you keep your head on straight, stay out of trouble and do the right thing."

"Well, I'm down here on some other shit right now. Excuse me, but momma I'm getting tired and something is about to happen. No more mister nice guy and playing by the rules. Only the strong survive, right? See, to me you are a weak link in society. You are the type of person that gets used and treated badly by people who don't give a Fu--. I mean don't "give a care."

"I know you will do the right thing when the time comes Patrick."

"I'm down here trying to be cool, telling these punks to chill out and I don't want any trouble, but they still wanna trip. I'm not a punk momma, and that's what they think because I've been trying to be cool, but something is going to happen, watch what I tell ya."

"Just do the right thing Patrick. That is really all I can say."

"Momma I've been thinking about you and I don't want to do anything to hurt you, so I've been chillin'. That ain't working, and these punks still trippin'."

"Well, Patrick you can home if you want to."

"I kinda do want to come home cuz I been thinking about doing some crazy stuff momma. I'm scaring myself. I really think I'ma end up shooting somebody. I need to finish my classes first though."

"How are you doing in your classes?"

"I need another alarm clock because I don't hear the one I got anymore, and momma these classes are hard. The information on the tests is not what they lecture on in class."

"I hope you are not messing up in school because if you do, do not expect me to help you. I did what I had to do with four children and no support. I know you can do it. Remember, I had three children before I got out of high school. You are older than I was and you do not have any children to worry about. I do not want to hear any excuses. I graduated from college with four children. I understand you might be having a hard time, but you know what I expect from you."

"Momma I don't need to hear that right now, you trippin'."

"I am not trippin'. You know what I am saying. I am letting you know right now where I stand before it happens. I am no fool Patrick."

"I'ma let you go. I'll call you later."

"I am not playing Patrick. You may not want to hear it, but I mean it. Do what you know is right and stay focused. Stop blaming the world when things do not go your way."

"I'm not blaming the world, but this world just ain't right. If the world was right, I'd have my father in my life. My life would probably be different right now if I had my daddy. Look at what happen to Chris' Daddy. Momma you and I both know Big Chris was a good person and Lil Chris is a good kid, why did his daddy have to die so young? I told you life ain't right. He died because of his heart problem not from gang banging or being out there in the streets. He always did the right thing, and you know it momma and look he died. Bad things happen to good people too. I can see if he was a gangbanger or a drug dealer or something like that. All he did was be with his kids and stay at home. So that be right shit doesn't work with me. Bad stuff happens to good people. I'm sorry for cussing momma but life ain't right and it ain't as simple as grown people try to make it seem. I'm doing what I came down here to do. I didn't say I was messing up in my classes. I'ma let you go."

"Patrick I know you will do what is right."

"Whatever Momma, talk to you later."

Patrick II is my oldest son. He has always been very mature, very wise, beyond his years. Every adult I know says he is too grown. They mean it in a good way, unless he challenges them too much. He did a good job of teaching himself how to drive. He is very smart and has always gotten good grades in school. He graduated from high school with honors. Sometimes he takes things a little too personal. He has high self-esteem, is very handsome, carries himself well, and is very mature for his age. He can also be my little boy when it is convenient. I have always kept it real with my boys and I never wanted them to feel they were the reason I was upset, crying, frustrated, or angry. Everyone who knows us can tell we are very close and continue to get closer as time goes on. Patrick reminded me that I am a good woman and the drama that Busta put me through has nothing to do with me as a person. He convinced me not to take it personal. He caught me crying far too many times to keep blaming it on other things, so I told him the truth one day. He understood but opened my eyes to different ways to evaluate what was going on with Busta. He clearly helped me realize that it had nothing to do with me personally and I needed to stop blaming myself. People are who they are. No matter how good they are treated by the other person. I am grateful to have a teenage son who is mature and has helped me understand situations I allow myself to get confused about.

Most people cannot handle it but Patrick tells it like it is. He has a different perspective on life that he understands and it has gotten him far in this world. Some people know if they are not careful, he could easily have a person seeing things from his point of view and changing their outlook on life. I know in my heart he will be okay because I raised him to know right from wrong and he will let his conscience guide him.

> *"There has never been, nor will there be, anything quite so special as the love between a mother and son."*

~Arthur Unknown

15

GO TELL THE THERAPIST

The receptionist did not look very friendly that day. I hoped she was not upset because I needed to speak with Dr. Smith immediately. I just had to see her sooner than I was scheduled. It was difficult to keep everything straight in my head. I told my boss I would be late, but decided not to go to work at all that day. Thank God for sick time.

"Dr. Smith is ready to see you now."

"Hello, Dr. Smith, thanks for seeing me early."

"What is going on Special?"

"It is my oldest son Patrick. He was very upset when we last spoke."

"What's going on with Patrick? Does he want to come home? He's in college right?"

"I use to talk to Busta about things like this."

"You haven't talked to Busta?"

"No, and I do not plan on calling him. I am working on handling the boys by myself. I do not plan on calling Busta for any reason. He will think that would be a way to get close to me one more time. I am not giving him a reason to come around no matter how good he used to be with the boys. I do not mind him having a relationship with the boys. They are old enough to deal with him without me being involved."

"Do you really feel it is over with Busta?"

"Yes, today I feel that way. Who knows what tomorrow will bring. I have been down this path before. I get caught up in the moment and remember all the good times and forget about the bad."

"Let's talk about what is going on with your son."

"He called me last night and discussed several things that might cause some trouble for him. For one, he is missing school because he does not hear his alarm clock and his grades might be suffering since the exams are too difficult. Also he got into trouble with some guys who threatened him. He mentioned wanting to shoot somebody, he seems so confused right now. We get into these conversations about doing the right thing. He feels like bad things still happen to people he knows who have done the right thing. I told him to come home if he had to. He sounds like he is on the verge of doing something crazy. I really feel like he might have gotten into something serious and he's trying to justify doing something wrong."

"You did not tell him that did you?"

"No, I mostly kept telling him to do the right thing and listened a lot."

"Good, he needs to make his own decisions because something will happen to make him realize that doing the right thing is better."

"He is very smart, responsible and wise beyond his years. He has avoided trouble this long and has not been involved in too many bad situations. He had excellent grades all through high school."

"He is old enough to make his own decisions no matter what. Keep listening; let him continue to vent, and do not make any decisions for him. He will come to his own conclusions. Sounds like he should come home before things get too bad. He called you because he knew you would tell him to do the right the thing and to come home if he needed to."

"Sometimes I am convinced he is totally right and he usually makes perfect sense. He brought up not having his father in his life."

"It sounds like he was pretty upset when he called. Why his father is not in his life?"

"His father and other relatives on his dad's side used to be active in Patrick's life until he turned about eleven. When we lived in California his dad's family would send for him to spend summer vacation with them here in Vegas. They also took care of Patrick while I was in high school. One day his aunt said another man claimed Patrick was his son and that it was unreal how much Patrick looked like him. It was downhill from then on. Patrick became very upset when he was introduced to the other man. Big Patrick and his family did not seem the same with Patrick after that. I tried to talk to Patrick's dad about it but got nowhere. We stayed away from them for a long time. When we saw them again things just did not feel the same. Patrick felt slighted and could not understand why they would treat him like that. I try not to blame myself but I was caught in the middle and felt like it was my fault."

"Do not blame yourself for their actions. How does he feel about his dad now?"

"He says he does not care one way or another about them. He feels like he never had a father but did not deserve to grow up without him. He often wondered if his life would have been different and believes the situation gave him a negative outlook about people and life in general. He gets sad sometimes and feels that life has not been fair, and does not understand why his dad was not around. Patrick used to feel like he was being punished for being a good kid. Yes, I blame myself"

"What did you say to him?"

"I listened and have asked him several times if he wanted a blood test to prove which man was his father. I have asked if he blamed me. I kept apologizing because I feel bad for him."

"Does he blame you?"

"I do not know. Years ago he said no and to this day he still says the same. He said that he could not imagine having a baby at fourteen and wonders why his dad and the other relatives treated him the way they did. I really do not know if he blames me or not."

"Just continue to listen to him. Let him make his own decisions. You talked about being in foster care before, tell me more about when you were in foster care."

"I believe Patrick will be fine. Like I told you before after I had Patrick I never lived with my mother again. Patrick and I went to Children's House directly from the hospital and were there for about ten days."

"Explain what Children's House is again?" "Children's House takes in children who need protection from abuse or neglect when they have nowhere else to go. Their parents and/or caregiver cause the abuse or neglect at the time. After that we were taken to a foster home to live with a lady I had never met before. My social worker never told me her name or anything about her. The good news was Patrick and I could live together. This was unusual since it was rare to find placement for a teen mother with a baby."

"I'm so sorry that you never went home after having Patrick. Was it ever an option for you to return home?"

"No, once they put the police hold on us, my mother no longer had any say in our lives and she never fought to get us back."

"What is a police hold again? I remember you saying something about that before."

"A police hold is when family services places a child in protective custody. Before the parents can have contact with the children or get them back, they have to get approval from the caseworker and see a judge."

"Special you are so strong and have been through a lot."

"I never really understood what was going on back then. I had no control over what was happening in my life and the social worker told me I would never return to live with my mother. She needed to comply with certain rules before we could live with her again. We were only allowed supervised visitation. Initially I was upset because I thought I should be able to decide where I should live. I wanted it to be my decision regardless of the situation. I had been taking care of myself anyway."

"Why do you feel you should have been able to make that decision? You were just a child."

"I had been making my own decisions before we were placed in foster care, and thought I was doing just fine. Eventually, I became grateful for being able to live under the same roof with my baby since we had nowhere else to go. My social worker told me my mother had not paid rent for two months but the landlord did not put us out because my sister and I were pregnant. Dr. Smith I wanted to cry so bad but felt I did not know her well enough to cry in front of her. She probably would not have understood anyway. When we arrived at the little white house with black trim on the windows, two girls were standing in the doorway. I wondered what I was going to call the lady. I knew I would never call her momma, not ever. I needed to know what she wanted me to call her. My head was down when we pulled up. When I looked up there was this very short fragile looking lady with long hair looking at me. She seemed nice and walked with an attitude that made me smile. I knew from the beginning I did not have to be afraid of her. She introduced herself as Big Momma. I laughed to myself because she definitely was not big. In a matter of seconds I felt relieved and the nervousness was gone I did not know what to say or how to act and felt helpless. My caseworker dropped us off and said she would call later to see how we were doing. Big Momma never said she called."

"You were placed with Big Momma without meeting her first?"

"Yes, I had never met her and did not know anything about her."

"Finish talking Special, you have been through a lot."

"The sun was going down when we arrived. Since everything was new to me, I was nervous and did not want to get to comfortable since I was hoping my mother would come get us very soon."

"So you had hope that your mother would come get you?"

"Yes, for a very long time. I finally realized she wasn't. I was with Big Momma until I turned eighteen. I had Donte' and Chris while I was in foster care"

"Was it a problem having the other children while you were in foster care? That is something else you talked about before."

"It was scary because there was the constant threat and fear that if things did not work out at Big Momma's house, we would be separated. I will always be grateful to my foster mother and the system for keeping us together since keeping young mothers with their children is not easy to do."

"So what was it like living with Big Momma?"

"Definitely not like it was when I was at home. I had rules to abide by and people I did not know took my freedom away from me. The other two girls in the house were very nice and helpful. I wanted to ask them so many questions, but was afraid to. They were both younger than me and one of them had been with Big Momma for a long time. She was very tall with pretty thick hair. She was a big girl for her age, and a lot bigger than me. She seemed excited about us staying there. She tried to make me feel comfortable. She even allowed me to have the room next to Big Momma's. She knew a lot about our foster mother and what she could get away with. I liked her because she immediately told me things about Big Momma and her children. She was fond of Big Momma but did not like some of her many rules. She had sad looking eyes that made me want to cry for her. The other girl had an attitude, looked mean but she was nice towards me after a while. Her body was bigger than the other girl's and she was tough. Because of her size she towered over me and that made me stay out of her way. She rarely said much to me in the beginning. She basically stayed focused on when her mother would return to take her home. She seemed sneaky and played by her own rules. She often shrugged at Big Momma behind her back. During our first night there I had an attitude because our foster mother told me I should not be crying because I had a baby. I could not believe she told me not to cry. It was my first night in her home, I was only fourteen and she knew nothing about me. Big Momma had no idea how I felt being in a strange place with people I had never met before. I put Patrick to sleep but I could not go to sleep myself. I lay there crying while thinking about taking my baby and running as far away as I could. It was such as silly thought since I had nowhere to go, did not have any money and was too embarrassed to call old friends. I was not ready to explain to them why I had disappeared or that I was waiting for my mother to rescue us from foster care. I got more and more upset while thinking I needed to do something, I had no idea what to do, which made me cry harder. I was so upset with my mother for abandoning my sister and me. My younger sister, Precious was in another foster home so I had not been able to talk to her. I wondered if she had talked to our mother since I had not. I felt powerless with no control over my situation. I had been taking care of my sister for a long time and they took her away from me. Strangers were in charge of our lives and told me what, when and how to do everything."

"Was Big Momma's home the only place the children and you lived?"

"Yes, and as time went on I started to learn more and more about the foster care system. After months of believing that I was living with Big Momma just because she was nice, I learned she was paid for allowing us to live there. I had no idea what it meant to be in foster care. I learned that she was getting a monthly allowance for my baby and me. When she first took me shopping, I thought she was spending her own money. I was so grateful, since I thought it was not her responsibility to buy my baby and me what we needed. Eventually I found out that she got a separate check to buy clothing for us. I added the amounts she spent and got more upset when I realized she kept what was left over. I grew more frustrated when she questioned my parenting skills and intervened while I potty trained Patrick. She went on and on about her grandson being potty trained at one year old. My son was eighteen months old when she forced me to start training him. I cannot forget when she made me spank him if he urinated on himself and made me sit him on the potty for hours. There were times when I would spank him for urinating or having a bowel movement on himself and after I spanked him he would walk away urinating on himself again. Being a young mother I felt helpless when she came down so hard on me. She often told me I did not know what I was doing. Many things that upset me were not taken seriously by my case worker or she usually felt they were unimportant."

"What do you mean she made things seem unimportant?"

"My social worker's attitude was that Big Momma had been one of the best foster parents the system had and in her opinion it was a good placement for me and the children. I admit that it was a great placement since we were able to stay together, but a lot of my concerns were never completely discussed or even taken seriously. She would just listen and smooth it over by saying that finding another placement would be hard to keep us together. I realize now that my concerns were not that bad, considering what children have to deal with these days. With the constant threat of my children and me being separated, I did not express myself much about what I was going through, what I did not like or how I felt I was being treated. Since I had that threat over my head, all I could do was grin, bear it and just deal with the whole situation. It was stressful knowing that every move I made could have jeopardized my being able to be with my children. It was not fair that they chose to separate me from my mother and they had all the control. Big Momma's children were on drugs and stole from my children and me. There was nothing I could do about it. Her daughter's children wore my son's stolen clothes in my face. Big Momma always promised to replace things, but never did. If I complained to my caseworker she reminded me she could move us but it would be hard to find a place where we could stay together. I was constantly afraid and frustrated. I still did not know enough about the system so I could not push the issues. From the beginning I never knew what it meant to be in foster care. I was never advised why I was removed from my mother other than she was on drugs. That was frustrating as well."

"Did you ever see your mother while you were in foster care?"

"Yes, but only one time, maybe twice. I do not even remember bumping into her on the streets. Our visit was supervised and I believe my mother was high on drugs. I begged her to get my sister and not to worry about Patrick and me. She never did. I did not know what she was supposed to do to get us back. For a long time I blamed the social worker for us not being with my mother. I thought she was the enemy because she made the decisions and had the power to change them. I just knew if she wanted to, she could return me to my mother. As a child, I did not understand that my mother's drug abuse was why the rent was not paid. That it was my mother's fault we hardly ever had any food since she sold our foods stamps to buy drugs. I later found out the social worker bought food for us and helped pay the utility bills before we were removed. When I turned eighteen we were released from the state's custody. My caseworker helped me get my own apartment, and it took me four months to get my children back into my custody. Once I had my boys in my custody, the social worker stopped checking on us."

"The social worker helped you get resources for you and the children before you turned eighteen?"

"Yes, my caseworker found a program that assisted families who were about to be evicted or were homeless. I had a choice to take the children with me, or leave them in foster care until I found a job and a place to live. I explained to my caseworker that I did not want to be separated from them at all, so she found a way to keep us together. Christopher was five months old and too young to be away from me. Donte' was growing and learning new things and Patrick was starting pre-school. I did not want to miss some important moments in their lives."

"So do you still have a relationship with Big Momma?"

"I love Big Momma very much. I will always appreciate her for keeping my children and me together and welcoming us into her home. I can never repay her for what she did for us. Her home provided me with stability during that time in my life. I did not have to worry about what I was going to eat and I learned to stop worrying about my mother. We remained very close. We talk mostly by phone since she cannot get around like she used to, besides my work schedule keeps me too busy to visit like I want to. I hate seeing her suffer which is what mostly keeps me from seeing her. We stay in touch through my foster niece Regail. She is an angel and loves Big Momma very much. She makes sure Big Momma always has my current phone numbers."

"Where is your mother?"

"I talked to my sister about her recently. We believe she is in jail. We prefer it that way since that is the only place where we know she is safe. We are always afraid to watch the news and find out a woman has died. We wonder if it is our mother each time. We have received so many phone calls about things happening to our mother. The worse one was when she was found unconscious and people kept calling to find out if we knew she was dead. I am never prepared for the calls from people telling me what happened to my mother. I am very angry with her right now. Every time she goes to jail, she writes letters about how she is going to change and promises things are going to be better. Unfortunately, when she gets out of jail she goes right back to the streets. She has been out there and doing drugs without us in her life for over nineteen years. She still will not admit she has a problem. To this day I cry, especially when she makes excuses for her behavior. I was very upset when I received her last letter. It took me three weeks to read it. I have always been there for my mother. Once I got my own place, she came to live with us. She did drugs in the bathroom and I felt there was nothing I could do about it. When we lived with my grandfather, she lived there too, and she stole from my boys and me. I was never able to hate her no matter what she did then or now."

"That is very good Special because you really do not want to hate her. You can hate the things she has done to you but you should never hate her. Why do you feel you should hate her?"

"She has let a lot of bad things happen to me and my sisters. She made us feel we were not important enough to keep us together. She never fought to get us back which made us believe she never really cared about us at all. Most years we did not get anything for Christmas because she chose drugs and her boyfriends over us. I still remember hearing my friends talk about us not getting anything for Christmas. I would never do that to my children. I believe she knew her boyfriend molested me. I get mad because no matter what, to this day I still cry for her and will always respect her even though she does not deserve that from me. I made sure my children know whom she is, although she was never around them. I still feel responsible for her sometimes and my sister and I would hunt the people down who hurt her if we could. She treated my granddaddy very wrong. She came and went as she pleased and stored all her junk at his house. Lately I have refused to let her know where we live because if she knocks on my door I would feel like I have to let her in. I would have been afraid she would not leave and I would not have the courage to put her out."

"Are you angry for feeling this way about her? You expressed these same feelings for Busta. You not being able to let go is an issue we need to work on. Why are you afraid to let people go?"

"With my mother I know if I turned her away and something happened to her I would feel like it is my fault."

"Special, your mother makes her own decisions, she is an adult and the decisions she has made have nothing to do with you. You do not have to answer the door and let your mother in your home if you do not want to. If she walked away and got hit by a car, it would not be your fault. Your mother has chosen her lifestyle she has lived and must live with the decisions she has made. You are not responsible for her at all. I am not telling you not to let your mother in if she knocks on your door, but you must understand you are not responsible for her. What is going on with Busta?"

"I really care about him. When we are together he makes me feel good about myself and he encourages me to be a better person. No matter how badly he has treated me, my feelings remain the same for him and I want to be with him. Half the time, I am not sure why I feel this way. Regardless of what other people think and say, I have to be honest with myself."

"There is nothing wrong with still caring for Busta so do not beat yourself up over that. Before our time is up, I want you to talk about the sexual abuse you mentioned."

"When I was about twenty-one, I had an argument with one of my boyfriends. He was angry with me for not wanting to have sex with him since I was not responding to what he was doing. It felt like I had an out of body experience. I told him he was lying about what he said he had done to me. I truly had no clue what he was talking about. I kept repeating that if he had done those things to me, I would have remembered. Suddenly I had flashbacks of when I was much younger. I do not remember how old I was. The next morning I woke up to my mother asking why my pants were down. Her boyfriend stayed over to babysit my sister's and me. Nothing else was ever said about it. Sometime later while we were riding in his car, he told me what he had done that night. When the car stopped, I jumped out. I could not believe what he had told me he had done to me. I felt sick but was telling myself he was lying. I had blocked the memory of the abuse and figured if he had done those things to me I would have felt it and I would have remembered. I told myself he was lying and never thought about it again. Something else happened to me when I was pregnant with the child I aborted. As far as I knew the father and I never had unprotected sex. When I found out I was pregnant he told me we had unprotected sex a few times. He would wake me up and thought it was okay because I never stopped him. I do not remember having unprotected sex with him. Once he explained all that had happened I felt like I had been raped."

"Do you have any problems now while you are having sex?"

"Not any longer. On a few occasions I freaked out and crawled up into a ball and cried for a long time because I felt violated. Those were weird experiences even though I wanted to have sex with my partner."

"It sounds like you blocked out what happened during the abuse and the argument with your boyfriend triggered it. It also sounds like if you are fondled while you are asleep you might block it out because that is what you did when you were abused when you were younger. You would go into a deeper sleep to block the memories of what you went through with your mother's boyfriend. You managed those circumstances very well."

"Is it good or bad that I am able to block those things?"

"There is no right or wrong way for a person to handle traumatic situations. You handled it the best way you knew how to cope and not allow it to get the best of you. Many people cannot handle devastating experiences so they either turn to drugs or alcohol. Some people use sex to act out their emotions. You were able to suppress yours. Do not forget, I suggested you let Patrick make his own decisions. When it is time he will realize on his own if he needs to come home to help resolve his situation. I would like to remind you that it is not your responsibility to fend for your mother. Think about why you feel it is. Continue to process your feelings for Busta and its okay to be honest with yourself. Maybe no one will agree with how you feel about him, but you should decide at what point you are tired of being hurt by him. He will more than likely continue to hurt and lie to you. It seems like he is not ready to give you what you are looking for in a relationship. You already know you need to move on and put him out of your life for good."

"Thanks for seeing me today on such short notice Dr. Smith."

"You are welcome Special, see you next week."

My phone was driving me crazy. It rang off the hook during my session with to Dr. Smith. I could not imagine what Michael could want at that time of day.

I made my next appointment and left Dr Smith's office. When I got home I returned Michael's call.

"Yes, Michael what is up?"

"Hi Momma, How was work?"

"I did not go to work today, I am fine. What are you doing?"

"I just got out of school. I am waiting for my dad to come home. Am I coming to your house this weekend?"

"Of course you can come over as long as you are not in any trouble at school or home. You know I do not care, Michael. Just as long as your daddy says it is okay."

"My Dad will say it's okay. Where's Chris and Donte'?"

"Chris and Donte' are still at school. You know they have basketball practice everyday. How are you doing in school?"

"I guess okay."

"What do you mean, you guess okay? That did not sound too enthusiastic Michael, what is going on?"

"I mean I guess, I do not know Momma, my teachers do what they want to do."

"I hope you are not in any trouble. You should be tired of being in trouble at school. Remember that is how you ended up living with your father in the first place."

"Momma I'm not messing up in school. Did I tell you my daddy be trippin' for no reason sometimes?"

"What does that mean Michael?"

"Never mind Momma I'm cool. I hope I get to come over this weekend."

"I do not see why not, unless there is something you are not saying."

"Naw Momma, my daddy be trippin' sometimes, that is all."

"Okay Michael, you know you have done a lot of things that make him clamp down on you harder, you have no one to blame but yourself. You need me to talk to him?"

"That is okay Momma I'm cool. I talked to Patrick last night, we talk everyday now."

"You two need to talk more."

"Momma, Patrick is teaching me a lot of stuff about life."

"That is good; he might be coming home soon."

"I hope he does. My daddy's calling me back, I gotta go momma."

"Bye Michael."

I have to clear my head after talking to Michael. He is the youngest and the slickest. He might out think me if I am not paying attention. He was born a manipulator and is so smart it is scary. I want him to use his gift of naturally being able to think quickly, process and evaluate situations the correct way. He has a hard time in school because he provokes his teachers a lot. He tries to play his dad and me against each other, but we stay ahead of him. He lives with his dad because he challenges me a lot and has been in trouble often both in and out of school. His dad is a lot stricter than I am. They are so much alike and they spend most of their time trying to figure out whose manipulating who or who is trying to get over on whom. I hope I did not come across too strong while we were talking today. I will call him back later. He is the only one of my sons without braids. His hair curls up with lotion and water and stays that way after it is dry. He is built like a football player just like his father and looks just like him. He will definitely grow up and make me proud as long as he uses being as smart as he is honestly. Once I realized his father could give him the discipline he needed and that he loves him as much as I do, I stopped fighting the idea of them living together. Every time I began to move him back home, he got in trouble again. Men can discipline children much stricter than most women. I did a great job with my boys but there are times if a man would have intervened, the results could have been a lot different. Once I realized that Lil Michael would be okay staying with Big Michael, I began to understand why I allowed Lil Michael to live with his father. I stopped being hard on myself and stopped trying to create reasons to have him come back home.

16

LIFE BEFORE THE DRUGS

Today I remembered when the foster care system took my freedom and my choices, stole my past, and projected my future. Foster care is a system to make children's lives better. It was supposed to offer me a better world to live in even though I thought my life was fine. I was surviving in my world. I did not complain about momma being gone or when I was hungry. I found a way to survive. I watched Precious reject the system and their rules. I had sleepless night because she ran away from every institution she was placed in. I could not let her live with us because I was afraid of getting in trouble for having a runaway in our home.

The caseworkers could not understand that Precious was a child who was used to abiding by her own rules. She came and went as she pleased, and refused to follow anyone else's regulations. A social worker she had never seen, picked her up from school and told her that life, as she knew it was about to change. There was absolutely no choice in the matter and it was a done deal. They expected us to accept what they had to offer with no questions asked.

I was so confused about a lot of things and discussed most of them with Dr. Smith today. I was feeling tired, lonely and unhappy. Working seventy hours a week was wearing me out. Granddaddy called and left a message while I was in therapy. He said momma might not have to go to prison. I wished they could keep her forever. The whole family felt better when she was in jail. She seemed to have nine lives and by then she had nine strikes. They just would not keep her locked up. I hoped she was looking better since she had gained some of her weight back. Momma was a very attractive woman before she got strung out on drugs. She had the perfect shape and I prayed to God for years to have a body like hers. She always kept her hair styled perfectly. Her skin was a clear caramel brown. I envied her and wanted to have her shape and look. When I noticed hair under her arms, I checked to see if I had any. I wanted to be just like her. There were many things about momma that amazed me. She was able to handle the good as well as the bad and usually rolled with the punches. We listened to the oldies and sang songs together. Our favorite song was My Guy by Mary Wells. We sang that song over and over, laughed and enjoyed each other. To this day when I hear that song I feel sad and start crying. Momma did not allow us to talk back. She disciplined us and did not hesitate to throw a shoe at us if we disobeyed. We had to be in the house before the streetlights came on and she was very strict about that rule. We knew if we did not obey there would be consequences that were no joke. Momma spanked us when we needed it. Our spankings reminded us that she was the boss. Early one evening when momma had company she told us it was time to go to bed. It was earlier than usual and we were not sleepy. I started making fun of her and to this day I do not know if she heard what I said but, she yelled, "Go to Bed!" My oldest sister kept saying she heard me. I was scared and did not say a word for a long time. The minute I told my sister to leave me alone, she yelled "Shut up!" That did it. From then on I thought she had radar ears. If we had not completed our chores she would wake us up in the middle of the night and made us finish them while we were half asleep.

We lived in a house before we moved to the projects. As a child, I did not know what the projects were. Momma said she wanted to live in an apartment for a while to save money. My sisters and I were fine with that because there were more people to be friends with. Before we moved to the projects, we got Christmas gifts and new clothes on every holiday. When we moved in the projects our lives changed forever. My mother was the best mom ever before we moved into the projects.

When I see my mother she weighs about ninety pounds. Her fingernails, toes nails and hair are very dirty. Her clothes are mismatched, the colors do not go together and her shoes are run down. She still holds her head up high though and walks like she is the most gracious woman on the earth and is wearing her finest outfit. She is still in denial about being a drug addict. She has an excuse for all her faults and has a rhythmic saying or quote for everything. I will never forget when she told me if it was not for her I would not be where I am today. She took credit for everything I had accomplished on my own. I remember one of her favorite quotes "I'm the creator of the maker and you came from the creator" meaning God made her and she made me so that is where I get my success from. She is stressing my granddaddy out. She should be taking care of him and not the other way around. Instead he is worrying about her and wishes she would get herself together. I can tell he believes her when she says things are going to change. He wants her to be the person she was years ago. Granddaddy has no idea what to do with her. He is calling me right now.

"Hey Granddaddy, how are you doing today?"

"I'm fine. I have a message from your mother. She wants some money put on her books for personal items."

"Granddaddy I am not giving momma any more money. She did not go to jail for a crime I committed so I am not helping her anymore. I finally realized

I do not owe her anything. She has never done right by my boys and me and continues to cause me pain. She writes letters full of lies and acts like she has never done anything wrong. She does not appreciate how fortunate she is when she is out of jail. She needs to experience whatever she is going through now to jolt her back to reality."

"I understand that. I'm not saying you need to take her some money. I was just telling you what she said. Soon she will be transferred to a rehab facility. She said she's made some changes for real this time and will prove to everybody she's a different person. Your oldest sister came by here the other day."

"Granddaddy she has been saying that for years now and it is the same old thing. I am not going to let her get to me this time. I used to think drug addicts could not function in society once they were hooked. I found out differently when auntie Renae got herself together. So there is no excuse for momma. I refuse to allow her make me cry anymore. I do not owe her anything. What did Dimples want?"

"She stopped by to get her mail that was all. I understand how you feel about your mother. I'm tired of her ways too. Half the time I don't know what to do with that woman. Just keep your respect for her."

"Granddaddy, Donte' is calling, I will see you later, before I go to my job at the casino, bye!"

"Okay, talk to you later. Think about what I said about your mother."

Starting a conversation with Donte'.

"Hey Donte', what is going on?"

"Momma, where are you?"

"I am on my way to get Chris so he can drop me off at work. Where are you?"

"I'm leaving practice. Can I use my debit card to get something to eat? Are you working tonight?"

"Yes, you can use your debit card. I hope you are not using that card too much Donte'."

"I'm not ma, I'm just going to buy something to eat. I did use it the other day though."

"You know that money is for your cap and gown, your pictures and your fees right Donte'? Why are you asking if I am going to work? What are you trying to do?"

"Big Maun and I got these girls coming over, that's all."

"Whatever Donte', you have some condoms?"

"Yeah momma, I have condoms but we're not going to do anything like that. These are some new females so we're just going to hang out."

"Whatever Donte', I love you and I will talk to you later. Remember you are signed up for the SATs in December and January."

"I Love you too, tell Chris to call me. What time in December, I know it's at the high school, but I don't know when."

"I will check my e-mail and let you know. Be good Donte' and do your homework."

"Alright momma, I did my homework already."

Donte' is my second son. He has stayed busy with sports, the phone, females and school since the ninth grade. He plays football, basketball and runs track. I feel bad for him because he is so short. He is up every day by five in the morning and usually does not get home until after eight or nine at night. He is self-reliant at times and avoids asking me for anything. He loves talking on the telephone and is quite the lady's man. He has long braids and a fair complexion. His chest and arms are very muscular. He is a cutie. He keeps reminding me about what he needs to prepare for graduation. It was the opposite with my oldest, Patrick. The only thing Patrick needed from me was money for his fees. He took care of his cap and gown, graduation pictures and everything else by himself. With Donte, I have to do all the paperwork, find out all the information for him and provide the fees for everything. When it comes to getting around though, he does try to give me some slack. He would only ask for a ride when he has exhausted all other possibilities before I started having Chris pick him up. He is taking his time about getting his driver's license. His main focus now is building up his muscles. If his cell phone would stop ringing, he could get something done. He always wears expensive clothes and shoes. I stay praying that he would get his driver's license and stay focused on school.

As for momma, if she gets out of jail granddaddy will start worrying all over again. I have told her a million times she needs to start taking care of him for a change. I hate to see him all alone. I do not want him to grow old all by himself. My granddaddy is a very loving man and will do whatever he can for anybody. He worked for over fifty years and has been in his home for more than twenty-five. He took us in when the boys and me moved back from California. He refused to move in with us when I bought our new home. He tries to stay busy, but I notice he is growing weary. Granddaddy is in his eighties, gets around very well and stays active. He does his own yard work, keeps his home immaculate and rearranges the furniture often. He attends Sunday services faithfully but I am glad he never forced religion on the children and me. He is strong but my mother's history has weakened him. She is the only child he has left and she takes advantage of that. I pray to God his health stays strong for a long time.

Renae is my mother's younger sister but they have different fathers. She is the aunt who was able to get clean and never looked back. Renae and my mother used to do drugs together. There was a time I believed a drug addict would never be able to function in society as a normal person. Renae has been off drugs for over seven years. She goes to work everyday, repaired her credit, has a good husband, and is a wonderful grandmother. I believe watching my aunt get clean was God's way of showing me that there might be hope for my mother.

It was a long night at work. When I thought thirty minutes had gone by, only five minutes had passed. I cannot focus on anything right now and I am in a confused state of mind. I hope God is not mad about how I am feeling. The customers were getting to me and I have started feeling lonely. I am frustrated because Chris is not answering his phone. I hope he picks me up on time. I need to take a long vacation soon. But where would I go and I am not sure who I would travel with? I definitely do not want to go alone.

Chris is late and still has not answered his phone.

This is so frustrating.

"Nikki, can you take me home?"

"Girl, I told you if you need a ride just let me know. What's wrong?"

"Chris must be asleep. It is not like him to be late."

"I have no problem taking you home. Girl, get in this car."

We arrived at the house.

"That is what I thought happened. See, the car is in the driveway, thanks Nikki. Do you want some gas money?"

"Don't make me cuss you out. No, I don't want any gas money, see you tomorrow."

"I really appreciate the ride, Nikki, I do not know how I would have gotten home. It is too late to call anyone to get a ride."

"I told you a long time ago if you needed a ride, ask me."

"Thanks, I will be at work tomorrow, you better show up too."

Nikki is a co-worker at my second job at the casino. She is a very nice person, and will go out of her way to help anyone. I like that about her because not too many people will sacrifice their time for someone else without something in return. Nikki will help people just because she can. I am like that, and feel a connection with her because of it.

Through her, God reminded me there are other people around who help others without expecting anything in return. As much as I do for people, it's comforting to know other people that are helpful and care, and not just talk.

> *"Life isn't about getting and having, it's about giving and being."*

> **~Kevin Kruse**

17

MURDER IN OUR HOUSE

As soon as I got in the house and situated I thought about my sister Precious and decided to call her. I hoped she was still awake I was feeling frustrated.

"Hey Precious, Chris was asleep and did not pick me up from work so I got a ride from my co-worker. I am so tired of working these two jobs. He has to stay up at night waiting for my shift to end. That is not fair to him, I know he is tired."

"Why are you crying and why didn't you call me?"

"I am just so tired. You know most of the time I feel like there is nobody I can turn to. It is a shame I cannot depend on anyone who I bent over backwards to help in the past. I have been there for a lot of people but I know I cannot rely on any of them. I started to call Busta"

"Come on Special, you need to do something about this Busta drama. It is time for you to meet somebody else. Until then you are going keep waiting for Busta to change and we both know that is not going to happen. That three foot tall punk will never change. I keep telling you to move on. Every night I pray that everything will be all right and that something good will happen for us. Did I tell you my lawyer took my case? Maybe that will be the big financial break we need. It might take a while but it will come."

"No, you did not tell me. I do not need to think about when you got shot in the head right now."

"Why, I'm cool with it. God looked out for me. I know there were several lessons for me to learn and focus on when I got shot. I know I scare you sometimes. Girl it is going to be all right, please stop crying."

"I was so scared. When I got that call, I thought you had been stabbed, I could not understand what they were telling me. I probably would not have been able to drive if I had understood."

"That was Black telling you to come get me. Everybody was yelling and screaming. For a while I was still able to understand what was going on around me until I passed out."

"When I got to the restaurant, I asked if I could get in the ambulance with you. Henry told me to let the ambulance go since you had been shot in the head. I do not know what happened after that, but I felt light headed then I hit the ground."

"I know, they told me you made everyone in the whole parking lot start crying. You were crying before you hit the ground. They said Henry picked you up."

"That was so scary and all kinds of things were going through my mind. I really thought you were going to die. I knew you had been drinking and thought you would not be able to fight for your life."

"I know there were plenty of people out there hoping I was dead. God looked out for me though, you can't stop a soldier. You won't believe how many stories I've heard since then, from you shooting me to me shooting myself. LOL"

"I still remember when I arrived at the trauma center. I asked the paramedic if he had transported you. He said you were going to be okay and that it was a miracle because the bullet appeared to have slightly grazed your forehead and it was like the bullet bounced off your head. I kept crying and thanked God over and over again."

"I was scared too, blood was everywhere and it felt like I had been hit with a boulder."

"I must say, Busta kept me calm on the phone while I was driving to the hospital. I cannot believe he did not show up to make sure I was alright."

"Stop talking about him. Eventually, he'll regret the drama he put you through. He knows how good you were to him. I probably would have gotten off the hospital bed and told him to grow two more feet. Stop trippin' about what he does and doesn't do. When I was in that hospital bed I thought about Auntie Karen being murdered in our house. Now, that is something to think about, forget about Busta."

"I have not thought about her in a long time. I know if she was still around, our lives would be very different and so much better."

"Me too, I know we would be better off. We would have never been in foster care and momma probably would have gotten herself together by now. Auntie Karen didn't play. I remember the whole incident like it was yesterday."

"I remember it too! I just had not thought about it lately. I kept thinking it was something you see on TV about somebody else's family not our own."

"I remember you, Dimples, Momma and me had just gotten back from the store when auntie Karen came home with her boyfriend, Jason and a lady we did not know. They went into auntie's room and closed the door only part way. They had been in the room for a while. On my way to the bathroom I was peeking through the door. Suddenly a gun went off and the lady ran out of the room yelling, "He's crazy, he shot her."

"Yeah, I remember. Momma jumped up off the couch from her deep sleep. It was hard to wake up her before that. She must have felt something was terribly wrong. Dimples and I started crying. You were speechless and peed on yourself. Momma picked up the phone, hit the lady in the head and knocked her down to keep her from running away."

"That mess was crazy. Momma stopped that lady from leaving. She hit her so damn hard she busted her head open. I watched Jason drop the gun behind the bed where auntie Karen was lying. Something was tied around her wrist and there was a box lying next to her. There was blood on the curtain. Jason grabbed a brown bag and ran out of the house. Remember you tried to run after him and hurt your ankle?"

"What was I thinking? What was I going to do? Get shot too? I was scared."

"I don't know what you were thinking, but at least they caught Jason because you saw which way he went. Momma went next door to get the guys that were paramedics to see what they could do to help our auntie. The lady was still on the floor with blood gushing from her head. Then the police came and took us to the station to ask lots of questions. They kept telling us that auntie Karen was okay, remember?"

"They were lying the whole time so we would calm down and give a statement. I kept praying that auntie would be okay. I was scared to ask if she was dead."

"I knew she was dead because while I was standing in the door way I saw her eyes roll back in her head and then they stopped moving. I wanted to think she was asleep, but I knew better even as young as I was. I remember the blood on the curtain and auntie lying on her back. It was scary. At least Jason went to prison. He murdered auntie in cold blood"

"Yea, murdered her is exactly what he did. Remember in court he lied and said our auntie shot herself because she was high on drugs. If you had not seen him drop that gun and that lady had not run out the room, there is no telling what stories would have been told. "

"It is a shame that lady did not serve any time in prison. She wasn't even arrested. She and Jason could have made up all kinds of lies. All of them were in that room doing drugs. I would not know the lady if I saw her to this day."

"I know, imagine if Dimples had to run into her, she would beat the crap out of her, shoot her, and then hang her. We know how crazy Dimples can be."

"Auntie was too nice of a person to be murdered like that. She was the sweetest person and was friendly to everybody. She spoke to people she did not know and looked at them with the friendliest smile. I remember thinking that I wanted to be like her when I got older. She always helped us when momma needed something. She never had any children of her own."

"At times I wanted to be like her too. I do not think auntie could have children. When I was ten years old she caught me shaving my legs. She asked what I was doing and told me a lady does not shave what Mother Nature put there. She told me I had beautiful legs and to this day I never shaved my legs again. There was something in the way she said I had beautiful legs that made me believe her. I spent days feeling like there was something beautiful about me after all."

"Stop being so emotional. It's over now, quit crying and go to sleep."

"Forget you, you brought it up. I will be okay."

"You work tomorrow?"

"You know I go to work, only one job though, I will call you when I get off."

Once Precious recovered from getting shot in the head, it did not take long for to fall back into her old routine. She prays every day and is a survivor. She tries to do right by people, except me at times. I am her punching bag. She does not have our mother to depend on, so she expects me to be there for her. She does not seem to appreciate me at times and takes everything I do for granted.

I did not sleep much that night and kept looking at my phone hoping Busta would call and just say something, anything. For some stupid reason, I needed to know he was thinking about me.

I started thinking about being in other bad relationships and being in that abusive relationship made me upset. I am a very strong woman and have been through a lot. I tried to keep my family together. I stayed with Ike because I thought no other man would care to be in a relationship with a woman who has three children. I lived in project housing at the time but managed to keep my children and myself from the neighbors that were full of drama. I wanted more out of life and searched my soul trying to find a solution. I knew I would not be with Ike forever when the abuse started escalating.

> *"I am not a product of my circumstances. I am a product of my decisions."*

> **~Stephen Covey**

18

SOME RESOLUTIONS

My mind was still on the abusive relationship the next time I spoke to my sister. Special is talking to Precious.

"Hello Special, what you up to? And don't say Busta."

"I've been thinking about when I was with Ike."

"What about it? Why are you thinking about that of all things to be thinking about?"

"I got through it. I am glad I stopped fighting back after the last incident when he knocked me out."

"You realized it had gotten worse and still would not call the police. When he first started hitting you, he had scratches all over his neck so it seemed like you beat him up. Then he became more violent so you wouldn't fight back."

"No, I did not call the police, but once I realized what he was doing, I thought it was best to never return.

That messed me up when he asked me to have sex with him after a beating. He knew I was not going to say no. He thought having sex would somehow fix what he had done and make it all better. After I left, I was glad I met somebody else. Each time we broke up before I never paid attention to anyone else. I knew my mind was definitely made up when I gave my real name and number to someone I had just met. I was tired and did not want my son's to think it is okay to hit women."

"Girl, are you alright? I would have beaten Ike for you. I didn't know what you were going through."

"I know you would have, that is why I did not get you involved. I appreciate that Precious. I need to see what is up with momma and your sister. I am worried about them."

"That's one of your problems, trying to be there for everybody. Be there for yourself for a change and focus on what you need to do for your boys and you Special. You got past that relationship with Ike, which was a big step in the right direction."

"Yes, if the shoe was on the other foot and what I went through with Ike would have happened to one of my friends I would have feared for their life. I finally woke up and realized how much danger I was in. I am very thankful I ended it before anything more serious happened. Ike is too large to treat any woman like a punching bag. If anger gets to that point a real man would walk away. I did not want to put my sons in harms way either. I am glad I moved on when I did, my only regret is not having done it sooner. Keeping my sons safe is a priority. It is not only about me, it is definitely about US."

"What's up with Busta? I know you want to talk about him."

"The same ole, same ole, drama. I have not seen him since that last incident. I feel lonely when we do not talk, but I have been strong and refuse to call him. He knows once I have cooled off I will be so happy to talk to him and I will be nice and calm since I had my cooling off period."

"While you're worried about what I'm doing, what are you going to do? Remember what you said when you broke up with him? You didn't want a whole year to pass and be part of the same ole crap. Special, nothing is different because you haven't changed things and neither has Busta. He definitely has no reason to be any different because you always take him back. Sex with him can't be that good."

"I realized that the other day. What we once had seemed so real, what is wrong with wanting that back?"

"You're still living in a fantasy world. How long are you going to wait for him to get himself together? There is no Special and Busta anymore. What the two of you had is over. Let it go Special. You shouldn't even want him anymore after what he put you through. You were good to him and his son. He lost respect for you somewhere along the way."

"Okay Precious, point well taken. I have not seen him since he was so insensitive towards me the last time we were together. I am done, okay?"

"Not to bring it back up, but weren't you staying with grandma after the last time Ike hit you?"

"Yeah, we stayed with her because she watched the boys when I went to work. Girl, I needed to go back to school. Patrick told me the police came to the house to question grandma about doing drugs in front of my sons. I think I told you this before. If she had not been babysitting they said they would have arrested her and her friends. Grandma tried to blame momma for the whole incident, but Patrick remembered everything. I could have used that as a reason to stay with Ike. I could not afford childcare and my choices were worse than I originally thought. I was stuck and trapped with little or no safe options. It is things like needing day care are why women stay with men when they know they should leave."

"You did what you had to do and made the right decision. I'm glad you moved on. Now get over Busta. You are strong and you are my support system so I need you to stay well both mentally and physically."

"Love you too, Bye."

When we first met, Ike was pleasant and did not show his abusive side. The abuse started after I got my own place. Before we had a child together he treated my two sons and me with respect and made us feel loved and safe. He hid his violence for quite a while so I was shocked and felt betrayed when he showed his dark side. All I wanted was to keep my family together. I was strong enough to survive that relationship because I had been through worse. What the heck was I thinking? A man of any size should never physically abuse women. If it comes to that, it is time for him to walk away until he has cooled off. Women in that situation should not ignore the warning signs. If his voice gets louder and louder and starts punching inanimate objects like walls and doors it is time to walk away because eventually you might become the punching bag.

I tossed and turned all night thinking about my situation with Ike. I had three boys who did not need to witness domestic violence. I am very hopeful that Patrick with his cool and calm demeanor realized violence is never the answer in any situation. Before drifting off to sleep my thoughts were all over the place.

I thought about Mercedes and her relationship with Koby. I cannot imagine going through this drama with Busta any longer, almost a year is long enough. It has been seven years for them and Koby has not changed at all and probably never will. I know I need to stay away from Busta. Both of our situations are so similar. I know it is a losing battle and in the end I am the one who will suffer the greatest loss.

I am glad I did not do anything stupid because of my relationship with Busta. So many times, I wanted to beg him to come back to me. Every time I thought about knocking on his door, or calling one of his women I did not have the courage and it would not have changed anything. My only outlet was to cry and find another way to get rid of the anger. Mean thoughts come to mind that are very devious and that scares me. My better judgment kicks in and common sense reminds me of all that I have accomplished and do not want to lose on someone that is not worth it. I have thought long and hard about ways to hurt Busta. I am glad I never acted on those thoughts. I kept chanting, I hate him, I hate, I hate him! It has been awhile since we have seen each other. With strength and fortitude I can accomplish anything. I asked God to continue to give me the strength I need and to shower me with His mercy. I hoped He was listening.

I was overdue to get a mani and a pedi. My manicurist is Taz who works out of her home. She is very flexible and that is what I need right now due to my work schedule. She is strict about who she takes as a client because she never wants to deal with drama, gossip or difficult people. The person who referred me to Taz knows me well enough and feels she would be okay with me as a client. We hit it off right away and talk about positive and uplifting things like our dreams and aspirations of being successful.

"Hey Taz I am glad you were able to see me today on such short notice. As you can see my nails really need to be repaired."

"No problem, what has been going on with you? My trip went well and things are being put in place for my business to take off. I am constantly writing and coming up with ideas. I keep a pen and paper by my side. Wait until you see my web page."

"That is what I am talking about. I always write down ideas too. I constantly think about my next steps in the right direction and ways to be more successful. The last time I was here we talked about you getting organized for your business."

"That is my focus right now. I want more out of life, I want to better myself and get my business started. Some people don't understand that some of us have set our goals very high and want to accomplish more than we already have."

"I am glad we think alike Taz. I am grateful for my job with the County but I know I can do so much more and better than my nine to five. Having my own business would be the ultimate. I know it takes a lot of planning and extra work but in the end it will be well worth it."

"Girl there's nothing wrong with us wanting more and wanting to better ourselves. If you were in the social class with doctors, lawyers, CEO's or entrepreneurs, you would realize that you don't have to settle for where you are now. I want my own business, the big house and the luxury car. I want a career that I have a passion for and a lifestyle that I can indulge in."

"You are right, and that is cool you think like that. I have a picture of the car I want posted on my refrigerator, I remind myself everyday that I need to make more money to get it."

"I am going to put a picture of the house I want on the wall. Have you seen those Green Valley Hills homes? While driving around with a friend I told myself that is how I want to live. Those are very nice houses on large lots."

"That is the kind of home I want to raise my children in. If you have no idea how other people live, you would have no idea there was something better out there. Some of us get stuck and remain where we are due to lack of exposure to any other surroundings."

"Exactly! Some of us are not aware of a better quality of life since we do not surround ourselves with new ways of living or different ways of doing things. I look at big houses and test-drive the Mercedes because one day I want to own them both. I am doing nails now, but I have bigger plans for my future."

"That is the kind of thinking I like. People get so involved in other things in life they cannot focus on doing better. A bad relationship can put a halt to all that and anything else you are trying to do."

"Let's not get into that. A relationship can change your daily routine and the way you think, if you let it."

"I will not get started on Busta today. I am done with that chapter of my life."

"What colors do you want on your nails? Or do you want the French manicure?"

"The usual, French manicure with some gold, black or silver stripes."

"The radio is jamming. Let me turn that up, Jill Scott knows her song "Run Across My Mind" is the bomb."

"That is my jam too."

"What are you doing for the rest of the day?"

"House work and taking the boys where they need to go, you know, whatever they need. I like my pedicure. My feet look so much better now that you take care of them. I will never go back to doing them myself."

"We all need to pamper ourselves. We always feel good when we receive a lot of care and attention. It can be something small, just as long as we do at least one thing to make us feel feminine and pretty. That can be wearing something that makes you feel sexy or it could be a hairstyle we love. A woman can put on a sexy pair of panties and feel like a star for that moment. We should condition ourselves to focus on the positive things in life. I try to change my hairstyles and wear the best clothes. When I cannot afford to, I compromise with something else."

"That is true. All women should start pampering themselves. That is why I refuse to go back to doing my nails and feet myself. I will wear my sexy panties to bed and my sexy skimpy outfits, even if I am sleeping by myself."

"Well, girl like always, it is good seeing you. I will see you in two weeks."

"I guess I will go home and put on one of my skimpy pajama sets." LOL Taz just laughed as I walked out the door.

No work today, just thinking and planning for what lies ahead. I very seldom think or talk about Busta anymore and that is a very good feeling. I am focusing on what is really important in my life and feeling optimistic about my future. Sometimes it is difficult but I try to stay the course in spite of having been there and done that. The routine gets old after a while. Going through break ups and getting back together over and over can be stressful. It is possible to become consumed with doubt, shame and frustration since a pattern has been established. Getting bogged down and stuck in a situation that seems hopeless can weigh heavily on our minds and hearts. Remembering we are much stronger than we think. Remaining true to our families and ourselves is the key to staying mentally and physically fit and happy. Relationships come and go but genuine friendships and family is what counts and should be cherished for as long as we live.

Only God knows why I still care. I do not understand it myself. I am glad the crying has stopped. I finally gathered all the pictures we took, tomorrow I will throw them away. Somehow, I feel stronger.

> *"Challenges are what make life interesting and overcoming them is what makes life meaningful."*
>
> **~Joshua J. Marine**

19

STILL HOLDING ON

After being in therapy with Dr. Smith for over six months, today I started calling her by her first name because I finally reached my comfort level with her.

"Hello Special, you look confused today, what is going on?"

"Rose, I really felt like I wanted to see Busta the other day even though he has not called me. I did not call him either. I miss his laugh, him telling me how smart I am and how he loves my body."

"What do you expect from him?"

"I will get angry if he does not answer the phone when I call. I do not know what I expect from him. When he calls, he usually acts like things are cool and he is ready to make some changes."

"Why do you think that? Just because he calls and you end up sleeping with him, you think that means things will change?"

"Maybe he does not act like that, but that is what I want to believe. I do not know, maybe I hope just because he called it is a sign things could change. I hang on to that little glimmer of hope."

"What are you hoping will change Special? You and Busta both get something out of seeing each other. You would not keep going back to him if you weren't getting anything out of it. It takes two."

"I am not sure what changes I expect. I do know that he makes me feel bad when he sleeps with me and does not call for days. He makes me feel like sex was all he wanted and he does not care anything about me. No woman wants to feel like that. I feel used."

"After you see him, how do you expect him to act?"

"For some reason, it is hard for me to tell him no. I want him to call me before he reaches the corner on his way home. I want him to tell me how good it is between us and that he missed not being with me. I want to hear that things are going to change and that he wishes he could take back all the hurt he has caused. I long for him to turn the car around, come back and hold me the rest of the night and tell me everything is going to be alright."

"Special, that is not going to happen. You should stop saying you cannot tell him no. I do not think you want to tell him no, that is why you keep seeing him.

You have to come to grips with the situation and know that nothing between the two of you will ever change. It is the same routine and you know it. Think twice before wanting to see him again. Concentrate on how you felt the last time you were together and about when the intimacy was over. Tell me about your relationship before things changed."

"Rose, in the beginning everything seemed too good to be true. We always had a good time and enjoyed each other's company. Maybe I am having a hard letting go of what we had in the past."

"Go back to when you first met."

"I was attracted to his charming personality and his good looks. Initially I told myself we would just be friends then the more we saw each other, I began to like him. He made it obvious that he liked me by constantly calling and asking to come over or spend time with me. He was very persistent which made it hard to turn him down. Our relationship was playful and we often started to say what the other was thinking. We seemed to have a lot in common and we thought alike. We have the same bachelor's degree in sociology. We both love children and hit it off big time. In the beginning I wanted to take it slower so I stepped back for a little while. I had never had such a connection that soon after meeting anyone. He made me feel in such a way like no one had ever done before. Just when I thought it could not get any better, we did things I had never experienced before.

Everyone said we were the cutest couple and thought we were married because of the chemistry between us. Our attitudes and personalities worked well with each other and I felt we were truly connected. We used to go to the movies and shows. We ate out often, enjoyed hanging out and talking for hours. After a long conversation, sometimes after hanging up, one of us would call the other back within the hour and talk like we had not spoken all day. Busta made me feel good about myself by telling me how smart I was and that I was cute. He often complimented me on my personality and attitude. No matter what, I still believe he is a good person. He is very deceitful when dealing with women, but he is a good-natured man. He is a push over when it comes to children and older people. Busta is short and not too much taller than me. He has an athletic body and stays physically fit. He smells good all the time and he always dresses like he is the star of the show."

"Sounds like that would be hard for any woman to let go of. That was in the beginning Special, and that is definitely not how things are now. Have you ever given him an ultimatum by telling him your happiness depends on how he treats you?"

"Yes, I tried that before, but I did not enforce it very well. I get so caught up in seeing him, I forget about myself. My focus was about seeing him, not how I would feel afterwards. I bet if I thought about that first, I probably would not have seen him anymore."

"What do you really want to happen between you and Busta? It sounds like you are not sure. You are holding on to the past, and do not know what you want for the future with him. When you broke up you felt you were ready to end it all. For some reason you will not leave him alone."

"I was tired of the lies and feeling used. I felt like I was thoroughly fed up with the games. His lies and him making me feel used was a horrible feeling. He made me feel like I had done something wrong and everything was my fault. Sometimes we made plans and he would not call or show up. I constantly worried about him being with other women. I made excuses for him so I would not feel so awful."

"So what are you tired of now? Has anything changed since you stopped seeing him? Maybe you spend too much time thinking about the past. Nothing will ever be the same because that time has ended. Too many unforgettable, but forgivable things have happened since the good times. Have you thought about what it would be like if you were together again? I think it is a good idea for you to think about that. What would a relationship be like if you returned to him?"

"Wow, actually nothing has changed. He still lives with another woman so he does not call very often now that I know about her. When he does not answer the phone late at night, it usually means she is around and he cannot speak freely. I know he has a lot of growing up to do and sometimes he reminds me of my children by the way he dresses and the way he talks. Continuing a relationship with him would be stressful. One of his women called me and I was quickly reminded of what I was not willing to put up with."

"So, do you want to raise another son, or do you want to meet someone on your level? Ask yourself what you bring into any relationship. What do you have to offer a man? What Busta would bring to the relationship if you were together again? How much responsibility would he take on and would he be ready and able to handle what you take care of on your own?"

"If I look at things from that perspective, I am fooling myself. He has nothing to offer me except a few stolen moments of physical satisfaction."

"You have been hanging on to something that felt good at one point and you will not let those feelings go. I think you are addicted to how he made you feel and you keep going back for a feeling that is over. You will never meet anybody else and move on until you stop seeing him. Busta brings your spirit down and he saddens your eyes. He makes you question yourself as a woman and makes you feel worthless because you know you deserve someone who will treat you better. Do you want a man to treat you the way Busta does? Or do you want somebody who is going to make you feel good about yourself all the time? Do you want someone that will be able to handle responsibility, and will put your needs first?"

"Of course I want all that."

"Can Busta truly give you any of that? Do not think about having fun and the good times. Think of responsibility and everything else will fall in place for you. If not, what will it take for you to stop seeing to him? Are you ready to keep him out of your thoughts for good? You must be honest with yourself Special or you will go back again and again."

"First I would have to change my phone numbers. I have tried not answering the phone but that do not work. I know that if he did not bother me, I would not bother him. Leo pride I guess."

"Take some time for yourself and think about all you have been through. Is it possible that you do not feel worthy of a man who can once and for all take care of you and your responsibilities for a change? Your choices are not limitless if you change your surroundings and focus on your priorities and your goals. Being around like-minded people would be a huge plus. You do not have time to create or mold a man. There are men that are looking for a woman like you. As long as you are holding on to Busta, you will never meet a different class of man. Your loyalty to Busta is holding you back. Think about what you have gained from your relationship with him. You have to decide what you want for yourself. What have you learned while being with Busta? What else can you get out of being with him?"

"Rose, I know I deserve better than Busta."

"Why are you willing to settle for so little?"

"Since being with him, I feel like I have become a much stronger woman. I have made personal changes that are better for me. I did a lot of writing when I was upset and crying instead of knocking on his apartment door, slashing his tires, or cutting him."

"So what else can Busta give you?"

"I do not know."

"So why do you insist on still wanting to see him?"

"You are right. That is a good question."

"Start keeping a journal about what goes on between the two of you. Write down specific details and feelings, both the good and the bad. Seeing it on paper makes it very real. Include the phone calls, when you see him, what you talked about, and how you felt before and after the conversation."

"I never thought of writing like that. When I am angry I only focus on what a fool I have been. If I do write about him I rip it up because I get so frustrated, and cannot process my thoughts clearly."

"Maybe that is how you need to see it to deal with the reality of the relationship. Nobody is a fool for caring about someone. But you are a fool if you continue to play his game. You don't need to be Busta's friend. No sex and no late night talking that could lead to sex. Without being in a relationship there is no reason to be his friend. It seems like sleeping with him is why you two stay connected."

"That is interesting because I am fine when we are talking and there is no sex involved."

"All your life experiences have made you a strong woman, not Busta. You have endured a lot and still kept it all together. You can continue to do so and one day Busta will be a distant memory of your past and your trust in him will vanish. Your children should see you with a stronger man who is living alone and who knows how to truly respect you for the lady you are."

"I never thought about the boys' view of the relationship. They know a lot about us, but there is so much I have kept from them. They really care about Busta. My children have never judged me. Patrick has told me he could imagine seeing me with a man in suit or a doctor who is well established."

"Maybe you should imagine yourself with a man in a suit or a man who is already established in his career. Sounds like Patrick want the best for you and realizes you do not have time to wait for a man to grow up and get himself together. There are men out there in the suit and that are educated that are no better than Butsa when it comes to women so don't be a fool for anybody else."

Rose and I have become good friends. I left her office feeling haunted by a love that no longer exists. I kept asking and begging myself to be strong and let go. My mind said to forget him but my heart kept beating to a rhythm that told me I still loved him. My mind said he was not the one, but I feel so empty when I am not with him. I kept allowing myself to believe that things would change but they never did. The only thing that remained between us was sex. When it was over, I would sleep alone while he was probably in the arms of another woman. Why would a woman settle for that? Since we broke up, there was never any discussion about future plans, no pillow talk or having a future together. I asked myself, what I want. What I know for sure is that it is time for Special to get back to herself before meeting Busta. I must get back to my exercise routine, saving money, educating myself. I have to focus on setting goals, and enjoying the unconditional love my children give me.

I am here again God asking for strength to identify and remove negative things and people from my life. I beg you Lord to help me end this thing with Busta for good. I refuse to go crazy over someone who does not have my best interest at heart. I know change will take time, but I hope it happens very soon. Yes I go from crying to venting to you, please tell me what has to happen. Please make sure the answer is loud and clear. Thank you God, I know you are listening.

> *"Ask and it will be given to you; search, and you will find; knock and the door will be opened for you."*

> ~**Jesus**

20

THE SETBACK

*"Growth is a series of mistakes, that's the
only way you learn."*

~Steve Harvey

My phone is ringing, it is 11:45 P. M. I wonder who it is and what they want. Maybe it is my granddaddy or sister. I hope it is not an emergency. Oh my God! Do not answer it. But, what if something is wrong?

"Hello!"

"Hey Lil One, what's up? Are you up?"

"I am up now that the phone rang, Busta. What is up with you?"

"Why haven't you called or returned any of my calls?"

"I have been busy. I have a lot going on right now."

"Whatever man, you had time to call. Have you spoke to Patrick lately?"

"Yes, we spoke recently. He has stuff going on besides school right now. We have not been talking as often as we usually do. It has been a couple of days now. I know he is not telling me everything that is going on in Bellevue. More than likely I do not want to know and I will never ask."

"I talked to my little homie. I told him he needs to come home. He's into being more than a student right now. Why didn't you tell me Chris has a got a 4.0 GPA?"

"We have not spoken for me to tell you about Chris, and Patrick will do what is right, you know how he is."

"You don't sound worried. I told him he should probably come home and he sounded relieved. He's been going through some bull back there, messing with stupid females, and punks who are trippin'. Did he tell you he almost shot somebody? I talked to Donte' the other day. My little homie is crazy."

"Patrick is grown now and knows he can come home, I told him once already. I am going to let him handle the situation himself. We both know my kids are crazy about you. You are just like one of them. How is your son?"

"He's fine; your boys know I'm crazy about them too, them my homies."

"I will always appreciate you maintaining a relationship with them. Usually when the relationship ends with the woman it ends with the children too. I am glad you keep up with them."

"My boy is crazy about you too, that's why I allow you to see him. He wasn't having it any other way. He loves him some Special. I'm crazy about your boys too. So what's up with you?"

"Not much, just a little business travel and working on a book. Oh, and I finally started working out again."

"That's good, I know you stay busy. I can't believe your still working two jobs. Girl you know you can work. I have to remind myself that if you can work two jobs, I need to stop complaining anytime I feel tired. And you are so damned smart. You showed me how smart you are when we worked together."

"Thanks, just not smart enough to leave you alone."

"Girl, don't start. I really want to see you, with that fine body of yours."

"I need to stay busy. You have a job yet? And where are you this time of night?"

"Naw, but I'm looking for a job. I hope something comes through. Ya, boy been sick lately! I've been at home."

"I hate it when you catch me in a good mood while I am not mad at you anymore. You make me sick. You know what you are doing. I had a speech already prepared, but now I can't even remember it. You make me sick."

"It's all good! Girl you crazy, don't start with that. I wanna see ya!"

"Busta please, there you go, do not start with that. I cannot ever say anything because you think I am going to trip. Whatever, and do not ask to see me. I am not messing with you."

"Why? You know our sex is too good for me not to ask. When I say you are one of the top two, I mean it, believe that girl."

"Whatever! You make me feel like that is the only reason you want to see me and you do not have any feelings for me at all."

"There you go, don't start trippin'. That's what I am talking about. We are getting along just fine. There you go trying to get something started. You should know better than that. Just let me see you. Remember the first time in the Lincoln? That was fun. You said you had more fun than I did."

"I do not want to talk about the Lincoln incident. I did have fun though. Do not try to reminisce."

"Why? Girl we had fun in the Lincoln. You snuck out the house, while the boys thought you were sleeping. I can pick you up."

"No, I am not messing with you like that. You better be glad I am talking to you right now. I am supposed to be mad at you because you did me wrong the last time we were together."

"Girl, don't act like that. And don't bring up old stuff. I left you several messages since then and you didn't call back. Let me see you."

"Busta please, I am getting ready to take a shower and go to bed, you crazy. That is the problem."

"Girl come on, don't be like that. You don't go to work in the morning."

"No, boy I am not playing with you. I am not seeing you. All you want is to have sex. You made me feel real bad the last time. You were so insensitive and out of line."

"Stop being like that. You know you want to see me too. I wanna see you. Come on girl. I love being with you. I'm not out there like you think. I am not having sex like you think. And you know it's not like that."

"Whatever, Busta. I will call you back when I get out of the shower."

"Call me back. I'll be waiting."

I know I should not let Busta pick me up, but I cannot help it. I know he only called to get me to sleep with him. When we are done, I will not hear from him for days. It is his way of feeling like we are still together. Not that he cares if I have somebody else. I will be fine while I am with him hell, I will be elated. I want him to just hold me, but I know what this is about. I am lonely and he knows it. I am going anyway, but do not understand why. My body needs to calm down.

Busta arrived an hour later.

"Where are we going?"

"I don't know. We got gas in the Lincoln. We can ride for a minute. Now, let me see that body girl."

"You are crazy. There are no more dark streets; they are developing houses everywhere now."

"We'll find somewhere to park so we can get busy."

"You so stupid, you make me sick."

"Damn, you're so beautiful. I love having sex with you. Girl you got the best there is and it's always good."

"Whatever!"

"Ooh Special, I can't believe it gets better every time. I needed that."

"That was too quick, what about me?"

"Oh that was good, girl you the best. Oh that was good."

"Whatever, you always say it is good."

"I'm going to call you okay."

"Yeah, yeah, yeah, bye Busta."

We both knew we would not call each other the next day, or the day after that. I just knew it, which is the pattern now. I could not even look back at the Lincoln when I got out, I ran towards the door. We did the formalities of briefly kissing on the lips before saying goodbye. My stomach was hollow and I felt sick. I wanted to cry but couldn't. The tears just would not come. I told myself it was okay to cry. But I could not cry. I lay in my bed asking myself why I continue to see him. Why do I continue to answer the phone when he calls? Why? Why? Why? With no answer I had to accept the fact that I was being a fool. I knew nothing was going to change. He got his fix until the next time he needs his ego stroked, so he can tell himself he still has me wrapped around his little finger. I cannot cry or pray about this one. I need to go to sleep. I do not know if I should be mad at myself or not. I cannot cry right now, there are no more tears left. I know I should not have seen him tonight. That was just straight up stupid.

I spent the next day doing everything possible to stay busy; laundry, washing my hair and cleaning the backyard. When that was all done, I worked out a little and cooked. I got a phone call from somebody I was not interested in talking to or spending time with. I lied by saying I was too busy and could not go to a movie with him. I kept checking my phone to see if Busta had called. I refused to call him. I was not ready to tell my friends I saw him after our last episode. Mercedes would understand only because of her situation with Koby. It seems like that is slowly fading. She does not talk about him anymore and refuses his calls. Working on her degree leaves little time to even talk with me like she used to. My friend Alexis would try to help me make sense of the situation and analyze it by processing how I act during my levelheaded moments. That is when I am at my best. When I agree to see Busta I am at my very worst emotional self. I get moody and depressed. None of my friends judge me and want the best for me. Precious would curse to no end, threatening to kill him, slash his tires or break a few of his car windows. She would love to catch one of his women and tell them what a cheating man he is. She feels he plays with my feelings and is nothing but a dog. The next few days were long and I thanked God for my two jobs and my children.

> *"With everything that has happened to you, you can either feel sorry for yourself, or treat what has happened as a gift. Everything is either an opportunity to grow or an obstacle to keep you from growing. You get to choose."*

> **~Wayne Dyer**

21

SEEKING ANSWERS

I called Patrick to confirm when he would be arriving here in Vegas.

"Hey Patrick, what time does your plane get here?"

"I'll be there at 5:30 P. M. tonight. Is Chris going to be with you?"

"No, he has late practice. We will pick him up after we leave the airport."

"You sound a little down, what is up with you?"

"I am fine, just trying not to think too hard."

"Momma you crazy, you been talking to Busta?"

"No, not for a while. That could be why I'm down, but I will get over it."

"Momma, I told you about that man, leave him alone. If he wanted to be with you, he would get himself together and come correct. He ain't ready, and besides, I said I imagine you with somebody on a different level, so let it go momma. I cannot wait to get back."

"Whatever, Patrick, I am cool on Busta, I have my plans in order for dealing with him and other things too. I am glad you are coming home, and whatever happened in Bellevue can stay in Washington. Spare me the details. I love you and will see you later."

"I love you too. Do not be late momma."

I am not sure if I am ready for Patrick to come home or not. He called me one day trying to reach Busta with a sense of urgency. The next thing I knew he was coming home. He has such a dominant presence in my house. I know things are going to change that might affect Chris. I do not want to know what happened in Washington, and I am quite sure I did not get the whole story. All I can do is keep praying that he stays focused when he gets home and he continue school. God please keep him focus. Are you there God, are you listening?

Let me check my voicemail.

(Beep) "Special this is Rose. I hope you are doing well. I need to see you in the office as soon as possible. Call me when you get this message."

(Beep) Silence (Beep) Silence

(Beep) "Momma, this is Donte', "I got a ride home love you, bye."

(Beep) "Baby momma, this is Chucky, your son is scheduled for a required parent conference at school today, call me back."

Damn it Michael, not again. God please help my baby.

I wonder why Rose needs to see me. I love talking to her because she has really helped me. I feel much better mentally since I started seeing her.

Little Michael had to live with Big Michael because of the trouble he gets into at school. Now there is another parent conference we have to attend. He has a hard time in school. I do not think he is challenged enough and his mind focuses on the wrong things. I wonder what he did this time.

"Hello Rose, what is going on? You left a message requesting to see me."

"Yes, I did Special. How are you? There are some problems with your insurance. I submitted a claim to the insurance company so I could see you a few more times and it was denied. Since I did not prescribe any medication for you they stated you do not need further treatment. They only allow so many visits if you are not on any medication. That is one of the reasons I am not going to accept patients with your insurance plan after this year. It is too much of a hassle."

"Does that mean I will no longer be able to see you?"

"After speaking with them they agreed on one last session, when can you come in?"

"What is your schedule like? I work a double shift the next two days. I am off after four today."

"My schedule is tight today. We will coordinate something towards the end of the week."

"Call me on my cell, oh I changed the number. I will call you in two days and we will arrange to meet, I have something to tell you."

"Is it something that needs to be discussed immediately, or will you be fine until then?"

"Yes, I will be fine, I was with Busta since the last time I saw you."

"Did you say you saw Busta?" "Yes I did and Patrick is home."

"I got some of the journal notes you dropped off last week and you did not mention that."

"I know I wanted to tell you in person."

"It sounds interesting. I wanted to tell you that what you have been writing has improved and has been very detailed. Have you read some of the things you have written?"

"Yes, and because I read and processed some of the things we discussed in our last session, I changed my number, and some other things."

"That sounds wonderful Special. You will be just fine after our last session. I have some things to discuss with you. I am amazed at how you handled your sexual abuse. We will discuss your mother, the children and what is ahead for you. You have the answers already. You are Special. Let's meet over dinner later this week."

"Sounds good to me, I will call you in two days."

"Special, do I need to tell you to stay away from Busta?"

"I will be fine Rose, I have it under control. Thanks."

"Special, you need to find some closure with Busta. You have a lot of unresolved issues with him."

"You are right. I do not know what to do to get that closure. I have been lied to for so long; I hope I can see the truth."

"Until I see you, focus on what you are holding to, besides how things use to be, your still holding on to something that needs closure and you must let go."

"I will Rose. I think I will be fine this time, but now that you mentioned it, I do need some closure, thanks again."

I am tired of talking about Busta. I know that he is not my soul mate. A soul mate would never do anything to intentionally hurt you, lie to you, use you, or cheat on you. I know I made it sound too good to be true, but that is the point; it was too good to be true. I was responsible for that type of thinking. It was just a fantasy I had been holding on to and I had to let it go. All that love in my mind was not true love. Love would never be built on lies. Heck, I had myself convinced. I learned a very valuable lesson from Busta. Now I know how a man should never treat me. If a relationship is based on a lie, it will most likely end the same way. I realized there are things that I have never done in a relationship because I loved the person I was with. I deserve to be loved and treated with respect. I know Busta was not capable of offering me true love and respect and never will. Too much damage has been done to change the way he has made me feel. I now know that was all the closure I needed.

> *"I've learned that people will forget what you said, people will forget what you did, but people will never forget how you made them feel."*

> **~Maya Angelou**

Several months later during the middle of the day Busta was bored. He was flipping through his cell phone and no one was available. His other female friends were still at work or not answering their phones. He decided to call Special.

I wonder what Special is up to. I haven't talked to her for a minute. Renee' didn't answer the phone; Shonte' is at work. Allegra's mad because I didn't call her back last night. Dashaun is at work too, and I am getting tired of Asia. She is getting on my nerves and starting to ask too many questions. Let me get ready for her to act funny, but by the end of the conversation she will be cool. I will start off by asking her about the boys and the conversation will be smooth. She is not mad by now anyway. She was cool the last time I saw her. She did not trip or say anything crazy.

"The number you have dialed is incorrect, please check the number and dial again. Wait a minute. Yeah right, I must have dialed the wrong number. The number you have…" Damn she changed her number. Let me call the house. "Please hang up, the number you have dialed is not in service, you have reached a number that has been disconnected." She changed both of her numbers. She will call and give it to me in a day or two. I know she is busy. I will call her work number. Naw, forget it; I will know how to get in touch with her when I need to. Forget it. "What's up Peaches, I wanna come over."

When I got home from work the backyard was flooded because I forgot to turn the pool valve off. The garage door would not open with the remote, my cell phone is not working properly, and my sister needs a place to live.

Why God, Why? Why do you continue to let these things happen to me? I am tired of all the challenges. I know you can prevent these things from occurring. My make-up is all in my eyes from crying. My eyes are red and burning. What do you want from me God? How much do you want me to take? I am not "Superwoman." Why are all these things happening to me? You let Rose have a car accident before I saw her again. I really needed to talk to her. Why God, Why? I am tired. I am starting to understand why people kill themselves. If I kill myself, I will not have to go through all this. Patrick's old enough to take care of Chris. Donte is almost eighteen. Little Michael is already living with Big Michael. I am really starting to understand suicide. It ends all the hurt and pain, the frustration and the drama of everyday life. I am tired.

Busta started all this anger and self-doubt. Why did you let me get involved with him? Why? Why? Why? What was his purpose in my life? I hate feeling lonely and empty without him. I do not know what to do about Busta. I truly wanted to be with him. I was everything he needed me to be. You know that I am already frustrated and then you let serious stuff happen that you can prevent.

I have tried to live a decent life in a respectable way. I have done everything that I was supposed to do for my children, my family and myself too. I understand that I have accomplished things a lot of women with one or two children have not done. I understand that some of my accomplishments exceeded women in far better circumstances, but I am tired God. I cannot handle it anymore. I work two jobs, I keep the house clean, and I try to cook and make it to my son's games. If my family needs me, I try to be there for them. I hear out everybody else's problems and try to help them. I am running back and forth from the schools, the jobs, and the store. I have to be responsible for everything and everybody by myself. I am tired of being the one everyone calls on. I am sick and tired. What am I supposed to do? I hate being by myself. I am begging you to just snap your fingers and fix how I feel. I am begging you to help me right now. I hate feeling like this. I have no one to hold me, to tell me they love me, and it is going to be all right. Yeah God my children are there, but that is different. You know I hate to be by myself. I do not have a mother to lean on. I do not have a man to call and say handle the pool and the garage door situation. No, I have to do it all by myself. I am tired and frustrated. Lord what do I do? Maybe you are mad because I do not go to church enough. I do not know what the problem is. What am I supposed to do? I read Iyanla's book "Every Day I Pray" every day. I say the Lord's Prayer often. What is it? What do you want me to do? Then, you let Big Momma die before I spent more time with her. Why God, why? I barely have enough tears to cry anymore. I need a clear answer. You know I do not like being by myself? Why? Why am I by myself? I treat people right. Please answer me. I never did anything intentional to hurt anybody. I never intentionally did anything wrong. I never committed a crime that I know of. I do not lie, cheat or steal. What is it? I need answers now. I need to know what to do before I lose my mind. What God? Why me? Why send me through all this? What have I done to deserve this?

22

GOT IT TOGETHER

"I am a woman in process. I'm just trying like everybody else. I try to take every conflict, every experience, and learn from it. Life is never dull."

~Oprah Winfrey

I got up off the floor, and washed my face. I did not like what I saw in the mirror. I noticed my blemishes were extra dark and my eyes were red and swollen. I called the garage door company to make an appointment and arranged for them to repair the automatic system. I got up and made sure there was no major damage in the backyard and rechecked the valve for leaks. I called the boys and left them a message that I was glad they let me know where they were. I was headed to the cellular store to see what was wrong with my phone. I contemplated what to do to make tomorrow better. I felt stressed, but needed to get over it and change my thinking and attitude. I looked down when I came out of the cellular phone store and my tire was flat. I paused, decided not to cry, like I would normally do, and called my good friend Coop. From day one, I could always count on him whenever I was in a pinch. Yesterday I would have panicked, gotten very dramatic, while crying my eyes out. Today is a new day. I did not focus on the problem, instead I calmly figured out a solution. I had no jack or tool I needed for the rims. I waited for Coop to answer the phone. I remained calm and thanked God he was available. I felt a lot better after the tire was fixed and I rode home feeling much stronger. I responded to a stressful situation much differently than I would have in the past. At that point, I decided nothing was wrong with my life and that I was very blessed. When life happens just handle it. It's your response that makes a difference.

> *"Release emotions of the past that no longer serve you. Connect with your generous and compassionate spirit. Be thankful for the growth that comes from forgiveness.*
>
> *Live in the present and with an open heart."*

~ Creig Crippen

I suddenly had an overwhelming sense of relief. I know that I have been through a lot and a relationship did not define me. Some people have situations that can take them to the lowest possible point in their lives. I know I'm stronger than that. Once I realized I was much better than I was given myself credit for, I refused to let it wear me down any longer. After all, I had overcome so much. Being neglected by my mother at an early age and suffering physical and sexual abuse by older men made me a much stronger woman. I knew I had done my part and promised myself to leave that baggage behind. What was in the past must remain there. I intend to continue to be strong and better myself. I want those that society sees and less than to rise up against the statistics and naysayers, learn to love themselves and know that they can beat any odds they are facing. I did it and so can you!

If you happen to take something personal from my story, told yourself I was stupid (which I was) then look deep inside and evaluate your situation. Hopefully, you have taken valuable information to uplift and guide you on a path that is right for you. Recognize my ways of thinking about Busta and don't allow a man to treat you the way I allowed Busta to treat me. If you recognize any of these characteristics I displayed with Busta re-evaluate yourself. It's about you.

I will continue to reach out to God for answers in my life. I never looked at Busta the same after that last encounter. I have so much to be grateful for and I know there are women and girls that are going through much worse. My story serves as a way to help woman and girls see themselves in situations and know that they can overcome them. No matter what perspective you have from the things I have been through, recognize if there is something you need to change about your circumstances.

Crying is my way of releasing my frustrations and dealing with heartache and pain. Find what gets you through your hard times and believe that better times are coming. No drugs, alcohol, or anger is needed.

"Cry so hard that it makes you laugh."

~Lynne L Jasames

I have always had a strong desire to write a book. I share my story to help others rise above tough times and know that there is always someone else whose struggles are a lot worse. I know my story has touched many hearts while helping them rise above their adversity. With a renewed level of understanding and a positive outlook, anything is possible. I have demonstrated that when the odds are against you, you can BEAT THEM! After every obstacle I kept going. I got back up every time I felt defeated. Those painful moments brought out the desire to change my circumstances around and never look back.

There have been times in my life I felt lost, betrayed, used, confused, and hurt. These emotions caused me to cry out from the pit of my stomach. The pain comes from people I love and trusted. The tears I have cried are from the things that have happened in my life during times the pain was so overwhelming I thought I had no way out and nobody else would understand. I chose to cry and look for better ways to be a better person instead of turning to drugs, alcohol, or anger. There has been pain due to the choices I made and circumstances I was placed in. There were times I felt empty and alone even when others were around. I took moments to heal and accepted my role for the situations I created in my life. I drew strength not from crying and feeling sorry for myself, but from making decisions that would move me forward. I would rather cry, work, educate myself, move forward, through my tears and find a healthy way to heal instead of inflicting pain on the people that hurt me. The path that I chose for my life rather within my control or without has made all the things I have gone through worth it. All the things that I have gone through caused me to become the woman I am now. The silent tears were the most painful. All along shedding tears for the nameless and faceless woman and girls with the same or similar circumstances. If just one woman or girl can draw strength from my story and connect with the hardships, pain and struggles I had to overcome then the tears are more than worth it. The state of mind and conditions I found myself in did not stop me from moving forward. Everything that I have gone through and all the tears that I have shed made me stronger.

~Lynne L Jasames

Vision

To develop skills in youth and adults to overcome adversity and face obstacles in life head on.

Mission

Through speaking engagements and mentoring, I help develop skills and attitudes in youth and adults to overcome adversity while seeking their dreams and goals.

Purpose

I reach out to youth and adults from a personal perspective helping them to understand that success can be achieved before, during and after a crisis. Using that premise provides realistic obtainable goals while focusing on changing attitudes and behaviors.

God Bless and thanks for your support. Remember, "It's Okay to Cry"

ABOUT THE AUTHOR

Lynne began to share her story of overcoming adversity when she saw teens and adults alike respond to her story. She wrote and published her first book in 2005 and has spoken to many audiences. Her most memorable speaking engagement was having the opportunity to speak for the Sister 2 Sister Program for Clark County Juvenile Detention. Lynne began writing and speaking to show others that they do not have to become a statistic. Society would have predicted that she would live on government assistance, and become a high school dropout who would abuse and/or neglect her children. According to society, her children would become juvenile delinquents, end up in prison, and have no education. Lynne and her children proved statistics wrong and beat all the odds that were against them.

Through her company, Jasamesinc, Lynne facilitated a 12-week Mentor Program. Since 2002 she has given motivational, educational, and professional speeches to a variety of audiences. Lynne was featured on Channel 8 News, has spoken to a UNLV Social Work Seminar Class, and was interviewed on KNRP Radio, X-Biz.com Radio and on KCEP-88.1 with County Commissioner Mr. Weekly. She has spoken at a CASA Light of Hope Ceremony, Courtney Foundation Teen Pregnancy Prevention, at an Operation Teen Pitch-In Conference, Child Haven, Alpha Phi Alpha Graduate Class, City of Las Vegas Correctional Facility, City of Las Vegas Department of Parks and Recreation, Valley View Community Cares Program, Community Counseling Center, and at DFS-Foster Care Training Classes. Lynne was written an invitation by the First Lady Of Belize to attend the First Ladies Conference at the United Nations in New York in 2014. Lynne is in training with Les Brown to be a Platinum Speaker.

Recently, Lynne has established another way to give back to the community. She is the Director and Co-Founder of a Non-Profit Organization: SUPAINC (Supporting Underprivileged Americans). Lynne has partnered with her oldest son, Patrick Clark II who founded the non-profit. Their aim is to ignite the talents and skill set of America's young people so they may become productive, healthy, purpose-driven community members. Lynne and Patrick increase skill sets in adult Americans through parenting skills training and workshops, mentorship and educational programs, turkey give a-ways, toy drives, back to school functions, talent programs, and much more.

Lynne is a mother to five sons and lives in Las Vegas, Nevada.

When the odds were against a 17yrs old, pregnant with two children, and in Foster Care, she beat them!

"Here's to the crazy ones. The misfits. The rebels. The troublemakers. The round pegs in the square holes. The ones who see things differently. They're not fond of rules. And they have no respect for the status quo. You can quote them, disagree with them, glorify or vilify them. About the only thing you can't do is ignore them. Because they change things. They push the human race forward. And while some may see them as the crazy ones, we see genius. Because the people who are crazy enough to think they can change the world, are the ones who do."

~Steve Jobs

Pain
http://www.strokeassociation.org/STROKEORG/
AboutStroke/TypesofStroke/TIA/TIA-Transient-
Ischemic-Attack_UCM_310942_Article.jsp#.
Vjs7yChM5SU

Teen Pregnancy
https://www.dosomething.org/
facts/11-facts-about-teen-pregnancy
http://www.teenhelp.com/teen-pregnancy/teen-
pregnancy-statistics.html

Foster Children
http://www.childrenunitingnations.org/who-we-are/
foster-care-statis-tics

Love Me or Leave Me Alone
http://psychcentral.com/blog/archives/2014/08/13/
signs-you-may-be-in-a-codependent-relationship

Momma's Way of Coping
http://www.thehillscenter.com/family/
dealing-with-drug-addicted-par-ents

The Decision
http://www.abortionfacts.com/reardon/
the-after-effects-of-abortion

Overcoming Sexual Abuse
http://www.pcar.org/blog/
common-victim-behaviors-survivors-sexual-abuse
https://www.rainn.org/get-information/
effects-of-sexual-assault
http://www.stsm.org/sexual-assault-and-abuse/
adult-survivors-child-hood-sexual-abuse

Domestic Violence
http://www.joyfulheartfoundation.org/learn/
domestic-violence/ef-fects-domestic-violence

Life Before the Dugs
http://www.thehillcenter.com/family/
dealing-with-drug-addicted-parents

Made in the USA
San Bernardino, CA
12 May 2016